ALONG SOME RIVERS

PHOTOGRAPHS AND CONVERSATIONS

ALONG SOME RIVERS

PHOTOGRAPHS AND CONVERSATIONS

ROBERT ADAMS

FOREWORD BY
RICHARD B. WOODWARD

aperture

Along Some Rivers:
Photographs and Conversations
By Robert Adams
Foreword by Richard B. Woodward

Front cover: *Sand Creek, near Denver, Colorado,*
1985–87

Editors: Diana C. Stoll, with Michael Famighetti
Designer: Wendy Byrne
Production: Bryonie Wise
Proofreader: Laurie C. Burton

The staff for this book at Aperture
Foundation included:
Ellen S. Harris, *Executive Director*; Michael
Culoso, *Director of Finance and Administration*;
Lesley A. Martin, *Executive Editor, Books*; Nancy
Grubb, *Executive Managing Editor, Books*; Susan
Ciccotti, *Assistant Editor*; Matthew Pimm,
Production Director; Andrea Smith, *Director of
Communications*; Kristian Orozco, *Director of
Sales and Foreign Rights*; Diana Edkins, *Director of
Exhibitions and Limited-Edition Photographs*;
Robert Stephenson, *Work Scholar*

Note: Robert Adams has edited these
interviews for readability and repetitions.

Along Some Rivers: Photographs and Conversations
was made possible with generous support from
Lynne and Harold Honickman.

First edition
Printed in China
10 9 8 7 6 5 4 3 2

Library of Congress Control Number:
2005933820
ISBN 978-1-59711-004-4

To order Aperture books, contact:
212-946-7154
orders@aperture.org

For information about Aperture trade
distribution worldwide, visit:
www.aperture.org/distribution

aperture

Aperture Foundation
547 West 27th Street, 4th Floor
New York, N.Y. 10001
www.aperture.org

Aperture, a not-for-profit foundation,
connects the photo community and its
audiences with the most inspiring work,
the sharpest ideas, and with each other—
in print, in person, and online.

TO ERIC PADDOCK

CONTENTS

To ask an artist to comment on his own work can be a welcome occasion or an invitation for trouble. Separate and yet intertwined, like a pair of entities out for a stroll in a Saul Steinberg cartoon, the art and the artist's words about it should, in theory, go arm in arm. After all, the maker of art is commonly regarded as the most trusted source, the ultimate authority, when it comes to detailing an object's formulation and adjudicating its meaning.

Often, though, artists are unreliable or tongue-tied witnesses if called to testify on their own behalf. Minor White and Harry Callahan were by no means the sharpest illuminators of their own creations. The wayward independence of the photograph itself, which has claims on the truthful and the real that the photographer may not possess, often keeps autobiographical remarks on the margins and may obviate them entirely.

Robert Adams is an exception to this caveat. Open to analysis and self-analysis, as articulate in writing about his work as he has been in the making of it, he may be the first photographer to have reached the summit of his profession after having earned a Ph.D. in English.

He has been an ardent defender of traditional values in aesthetics, unafraid to promote a term like "beauty" as an aspirational virtue. His anger and disappointment with his own country, particularly over its reckless stewardship of lands in the American West, have been expressed repeatedly in images as well as words.

Not since Ansel Adams has there been a photographer of his stature who was also such a committed environmental activist.

The voice in the interviews gathered here is no less cultivated and urgent, although it is perhaps more relaxed than what we're accustomed to. Even a seasoned appreciator of his work, of which there are now many, worldwide, will be surprised that he is fond of quoting Groucho Marx ("I'd like the West better if it were in the East") and Fran Lebowitz ("I write so slowly I could write with my own blood and not hurt myself"). The formal discretion, tenderness, and moral fiber of the many other writers he cites here—Robert Frost, Mary Oliver, Wendell Berry, Edward Abbey—seem to mesh easily with what we have gleaned about his sensibility with only the work as evidence. That he should now prefer Dorothea Lange's more openhearted photographs to those of Walker Evans, and that he should confess this as a heresy, makes perfect sense.

The photographs here of riverbanks, structures that shape and are shaped by water, embody the Adams aesthetic. Few other artists would be bothered to examine so closely the vitality of this distinct terrain, overlooked as we gaze elsewhere in search of loftier testaments to nature's majesty. In his conversational style, in the writers he admires, and in his approach to photographing the world, there is a notable absence of photographic grandiloquence and artistic rhetoric.

It is only after decades of marveling at his body of pictures, collected in book after book and edited with his wife, Kerstin, that the depth of his convictions and the eloquence of his plain truths, slantingly told, has become apparent. Like all of us, he has been shaped by words and, as a former English professor, perhaps owes a particular allegiance to their powers of persuasion. But these revealing conversations with one of America's finest artists only accentuate how much of him was already revealed in the photographs.

—RICHARD B. WOODWARD

PREFACE

There aren't many big rivers in the American West, but there are a satisfying number of washes, creeks, and irrigation ditches, the roots and branches of rivers.

Should I, having photographed this landscape, try to talk about it? By what right or obligation? Perhaps only by the privilege of having seen the West when it was more open, so that nothing that has happened since then, no matter how bad, can entirely obscure its promise.

R.A., 2005

ABOUT
Cottonwoods
with
Constance Sullivan

CONSTANCE SULLIVAN: You've lived and worked in the American West for many years. Do you live there so that you can photograph it, or do you photograph it because you happen to live there?

ROBERT ADAMS: Do I detect in that question an echo of the Marx Brothers line, "I'd like the West better if it were in the East"? [laughs] I love the West as a place to both live and work. My goal as a photographer is to see it clearly enough, right where it is, to love it even more.

CS: Is there a suggestion in your answer, nonetheless, that photography might be part of a lover's quarrel?

RA: Yes, I'll admit to that. When I was young, I went away to school in Los Angeles, a place which even then wasn't part of the West, and when I came back to Colorado I found that some of Los Angeles had come to Colorado. It hurt. Photography eventually became a way to look for a reconciliation. That began when the college where I was teaching English held a conference about the Western landscape. I'd been making pictures of rural areas, in the manner of Ansel Adams, but the conference organizers asked me to make documentary pictures of the city of Colorado Springs, which was growing rapidly. I did so, and was surprised. The scenes were frightening, but one or two had about them an unexpected beauty. I couldn't account for it. From that point on, I felt I had some exploring to do.

CS: Are your photographs concerned with environmental issues, or are they primarily about your aesthetic vision?

RA: Content and aesthetics are inseparable. And in any case, I've always wanted to do more than one thing at a time. Lewis Hine

From Cottonwoods: Photographs by Robert Adams *(Washington, D.C.: Smithsonian Institution Press, 1994).*

said that he hoped to show what was wrong so that we would try to change it, and what was right so that we could take comfort from it. I don't often achieve that, but the two goals seem appropriate to me.

CS: How do you try to reach those goals?

RA: By refusing to cull away evidence of our abuse of the land and of each other. And then by refusing to turn away from what artists have traditionally celebrated in life—beauty. By which I mean form. The chief consolation in paintings by Cézanne and Edward Hopper, for instance, seems to me to be a peace that derives from the wholeness that the artists see in life and mirror in their work.

CS: Has the way you approach your work changed significantly over the past thirty years?

RA: I continue to try, as I have from the start, to be as direct as possible, and in that sense I think there has been a continuity of style. But of course one's understanding of life changes some. Mary Oliver's lines seem perfect to me now: "There are so many stories, / more beautiful than answers."

CS: Do you decide what the subject matter of your pictures will be before you begin working on a project, or does that evolve out of the work?

RA: Projects evolve in response to countless discoveries about the way light falls on particular houses or streets or people or cars or mesas . . . the discoveries are most likely made, I think, when I feel at home. Lewis Baltz said to me once that he believed he took sucker shots when he visited a place the first time. That's been my experience too. Though this isn't to endorse the alleged operating principle of the British conservative party: "Never do anything for the first time."

CS: But why do you feel that you have to be familiar with a place in order to do your best work there?

RA: Because what I'm after are characteristic views, and I can't know if a view is characteristic until I've seen a place again and again, through all kinds of hours and seasons.

CS: Trees are central to many of your photographs. What makes them so appealing as subjects?

RA: Trees smell good, feel good, sound good, and look good. And as if that weren't enough, they point beyond themselves.

CS: You've been photographing cottonwood trees for a long while. Do you usually work exclusively on one subject, or on a number of projects at the same time?

RA: Usually on one at a time, though I happen to be completing a half-dozen things right now.

CS: Do you photograph every day?

RA: No, unfortunately, I haven't photographed for two years.

CS: With what have you been occupied?

RA: Making books.

CS: Is book publishing something that you feel you must do?

RA: Yes, I suppose, because I usually work in units of pictures, because I try to reach a diverse audience, and because I know, having lived on the edge of the world, how important books can be. I learned to photograph mostly by studying books, and I try now to keep up through books.

CS: You also write about photography.

RA: That began partly out of necessity. Few publishers will consider doing books without text, and few writers are comfortable writing about pictures. John Szarkowski wrote a wonderful essay for *The New West*, but there's a limit to how much one can plague a man!

CS: When did you decide that you were a photographer?

RA: You mean when did I feel I could stop apologizing for doing it? Probably when I was fortunate enough to sell prints to the Museum of Modern Art and the Metropolitan Museum of Art. I still remember the day I got the letter from the Modern. I remember standing on a hill in Colorado Springs, with the letter in my pocket, enjoying the view all the way south a hundred miles to the Spanish Peaks. I'd bought a doughnut, and it was the best doughnut I ever ate.

CS: Are there things that are intrinsically more interesting than others to photograph?

RA: Stieglitz said that "all true things are equal," and I believe that. Though I also believe that the more true things you can get into one picture, especially if those things seem contradictory, the better the picture is likely to be.

CS: Is there a landscape or subject that you fantasize about photographing?

RA: I'd like to photograph in animal shelters. And, if I had the courage, in factory farms.

CS: What is the origin of the piece of bark on the wall next to your kitchen table?

RA: It came from a cottonwood that I'd been photographing, and that one day I found cut down. The fragment is peaceful in the light from the window. It reminds Kerstin and me of summer afternoons . . . of shade, white clouds, birds. . . .

CS: Willa Cather wrote in *The Song of the Lark*, which is set on the Colorado plains, that cottonwoods are "wind-loving trees . . . whose roots are always seeking water and whose leaves are always talking about it, making the sound of rain." That seems an especially beautiful way of describing their promise.

RA: I think her memory of that sound helped her all her life.

CS: Some of your photographs record, though, a landscape that appears not only to be arid but to be dying.

RA: All the pictures were made in Colorado along the eastern edge of the Rockies, a geography where our sense of stewardship has nearly collapsed. A landscape where, for example, we're building new suburbs that depend on aquifers, which will be exhausted within one human lifetime.

CS: Your concerns include, then, desertification, deforestation, pollution, and overpopulation.

RA: All those things, but with overpopulation at the head of the list, because overpopulation, together with our tragic propensity for evil, accounts for most of the rest of what has gone wrong.

CS: Do you see those larger problems when you look at specific trees?

RA: Sometimes. I often think of a line by Edward Thomas: "Trees and us—imperfect friends." Cottonwoods have been our friends for a long while. The Arapaho believed, for instance, that the stars came from cottonwoods, from the glistening sap at the joints of twigs. The Hidatsa believed that the shade from cottonwoods was healing. Everything about the tree, in fact, struck Native Americans as beneficent. They saw that even their horses survived the winter by foraging its inner bark. As, for that matter, did horses belonging to whites. And in other seasons immigrant wagon trains followed along from one grove to the next, with cottonwoods serving as landmarks, shelter, and fuel. But the human side of this friendship has weakened. Agribusiness now wages war on cottonwoods because the trees compete for water, and suburban developers replace them with conveniently small but ecologically disruptive species like Russian olive. Main Street in Longmont used to be lined with cottonwoods, but they were all cut down.

CS: Your pictures seem, nonetheless, quiet.

RA: I hope so. But when I'm without a camera I can be angry. Henry Beetle Hough tells a funny story about a woman on Martha's Vineyard who got so upset with an over-zealous tree trimmer that she made him nail a branch back on. I understand that feeling. And I try to write letters, though I don't do enough of what helps the most, which is to go to meetings. I admire people with the discipline and wisdom for that. My father is such a person, as is my sister Carolyn.

CS: Is there any consolation in the craft of photography? Do you, for example, use Ansel Adams's "zone system"? Do you enjoy darkroom work?

RA: I'm interested in craft to the extent that it allows me to be clear about the subject. I do often adjust exposure with development, though not as precisely as did Ansel Adams. I admire him, incidentally. He cared, he was generous, and he admitted to having a good time. He also made some pictures by which we all judge our efforts.

CS: In the early 1970s you photographed the same cottonwood over and over. Why?

RA: I first saw the tree one summer morning when it was full of children and birds. It was like a scene from Blake. In the fall, however, developers graded over the irrigation ditch that sustained the tree, and within a year it died. Cottonwoods can seem human—they seem to rejoice, and they seem to suffer. But they also seem to know a stillness that we can't experience, at least not for long. Maybe we are not even supposed to, given our minds and consciences. But the example of trees does suggest a harmony for which it seems right to dream. A friend, a Native American, told me recently that the Lakota refer to the cottonwood as "the dreaming tree," a place for visions.

CS: Your work has been called "an anatomy of Southwestern melancholy." Is that an accurate summation?

RA: I'd like to think not, but of course it isn't for me to say. I do believe that artists are obliged, like everyone else, to try to find their way to affirmation. The phrase "an anatomy of South-western melancholy" usefully underlines a problem though: as Edward Abbey wrote, the West is now populated by phantoms "dying of nostalgia and bitterness." Is that our fate, the fate of everyone with a memory? He went on to say that you could hear the phantoms "shivering, chattering among the leaves of the old dry mortal cottonwoods," though in another book he compared the sound of the leaves to "the murmur of distant water." Perhaps both metaphors are true. Perhaps our disillusionment is an end and a beginning.

CS: What is your basis of hope?

RA: I don't have an easy answer. I want to be hopeful if I can also be truthful. With respect to the likely future of the West and of the planet, I don't know anything more than what observation and reason tells us. But I also believe that we, who are small and have limited understanding, can celebrate the promise—the long-term promise—that is inherent in nature's beauty. And I am encouraged by other people's caring. Even by the caring of those who aren't literally standing next to us. By Edward Abbey, for instance, who became more resolute as he got older, at the same time as he became more gentle. And by the example of William Stafford's life and work. I can't give up if I remember such individuals and what they did. Thomas Worthington Whittredge, for instance, who belonged to the Hudson River School, also painted views of cottonwoods near here in the 1860s and '70s. He loved Colorado light. I enjoy imagining him working there under the trees along the Platte. His pictures remind me of lines by Theodore Roethke: "Whatever was, still is / Says a song tied to a tree."

ABOUT
WHAT WE BOUGHT
WITH
THOMAS WESKI

THOMAS WESKI: Your home is filled with books and pictures and boat models. What is your interest in boats?

ROBERT ADAMS: It's a little crazy, isn't it, here in the semi-arid Southwest. But I've loved boats since I was a boy. They're houses on water, where the builders had to be respectful or the houses would sink. And so the houses are beautiful.

TW: What is the current condition of Denver, twenty-one years after the pictures in the exhibition were made? Have the problems that the pictures forecast been ameliorated?

RA: Denver and Colorado in general are once again under-going chaotic development. The population of the state grew by 11 percent in the first three and a half years of this decade (that is the most recent period for which there are statistics). Some foresee a third of the Colorado plains covered by development by the year 2020.

TW: How do the pictures in the exhibition relate to the rest of your work?

RA: They were taken just five years after I began trying to document the suburban landscape. They were made possible by a fellowship that gave me a year of freedom, by the energy of youth, and by the fact that the people in the city and suburbs were not yet hostile.
   The pictures were also facilitated by my belief then that we could avert disaster, that a significant part of the landscape could be saved.
   And the pictures were made possible by beliefs that I still hold— that it is nearly always useful, for example, to tell the truth, if not

A conversation held in Longmont, Colorado, at the kitchen table, in preparation for the publication and exhibition of What We Bought: The New World, *1995. Thomas Weski was at that time the Curator of Photography at the Sprengel Museum in Hanover, Germany.*

because it changes society, then because it allows us to change ourselves as individuals, to accept what we must. And the pictures reflect my continuing conviction that, no matter how hard life is, the landscape is beautiful. The light. Even over a shopping center.

TW: How would you respond to those who contend that there is really nothing wrong with growth as it is recorded in these pictures?

RA: I've noticed that most developers don't live in their own new developments. Those of us who have to try to live in their creation discover what Wendell Berry meant when he said that "growth is inescapably shrinking us."

TW: Of what practical use is landscape photography?

RA: In a way, none. The place itself is always more remarkable than any picture of it. A picture is just an attempt to acknowledge the sufficiency of the place.

But each of us keeps losing track of that sufficiency. Bitterness accrues from what appears to be the triumph of chaos, and that leads to nihilism. Art has traditionally been the intuition, however incomplete, of a larger perspective, one that allows hope.

TW: You have an interest in motion pictures. Have films influenced your work as a still photographer?

RA: Many of the filmmakers I admire are the quiet ones, Yasujiro Ozu and Eric Rohmer, for example. They've convinced me that you don't have to move frantically in order to explore the center of life. Though the movie-maker who visually impressed me the most in the 1960s and '70s was very different—Jean-Luc Godard. There are scenes from his black-and-white films that remain with me even now. Raoul Coutard, Godard's cameraman, said in an interview in *Cahiers du cinema* that natural light is always beautiful. His films prove it.

TW: Are there subjects for which still photography is unsuited?

RA: Still photography by its nature can't register noise, which is one of the defining elements in our current crisis. Silence is space, and noise robs us of that. I've never seen a still photograph that effectively addresses the problem.

TW: Which artists have been most important to you?

RA: I sometimes think that most important has been the painter Edward Hopper. He is the key to the feel of the United States. To the light and space. To the beauty of half-developed places. And to the loneliness.

    Hopper's pictures remind me of an observation by Georges Rouault: "Light is tragic." Hopper's pictures are as troubling, intense, and finally as affirmative as old tragedy.

TW: Do you pay much attention to what is happening in contemporary art?

RA: No. I suppose because of my commitment to subject matter, because of my lack of interest in process, and because of my conviction that useful pictures don't start from ideas. They start from seeing.

TW: As a photographer, do you feel part of a community?

RA: Yes, though ironically it seems to me that in America, and perhaps in Western Europe, artists find themselves now in a position not unlike that of artists in the Soviet Union twenty years ago. Except that here the censorship is economic, the network of colleagues is thinner, and the route of escape unknown.

TW: Do you think you will ever photograph Denver as extensively again?

RA: I believe that art should, in the last analysis, be encouraging. Which means, because lies are finally discouraging, that it should be affirmative even about what has happened to *most* of the landscape. I'm not sure I'm equal to that in Denver anymore.

TW: What do you think is the future of the American West?

RA: As a land of space, where one might be alone with one's thoughts, I don't think it has a future—just a history.

Yes, there are tiny shards of the mythic West that remain, but the West that transformed generations was neither small nor fragmented.

As a region, the American West seems to me now as worn out as Switzerland.

A funny Jewish country singer from west Texas, Kinky Friedman, has a great line: "When the horse dies, get off." That's where we are now in the West. We need to get off and discover how to make a life without the horse.

Every July in Cheyenne, a hundred miles north from here, they stage a week-long festival called "Frontier Days." It is one of the largest rodeos in the United States, but it is meaningless—nothing more than a meeting of big-time athletics with animal abuse. There is, of course, a new frontier, but celebrations of the old frontier are an obstacle to recognizing it.

TW: If the pictures in *What We Bought* record mostly society's failure, what would success look like?

RA: Wendell Berry, in his book about the painter Harlan Hubbard, wrote that Hubbard's landscapes of farm country along the Ohio River in the 1920s and '30s recorded "the people and their works occupying their places as the trees do." I think that is what success would look like—occupying the land as trees do. What we're after is what the writer Frank Waters said he found at his home in the Sangre de Cristo mountains north of Taos. "There," he wrote, "I have a speaking acquaintance with the trees."

ABOUT
PRIORITIES

WITH

MEMBERS OF THE
SAN FRANCISCO MUSEUM
OF MODERN ART

I think we begin conversations like this partly out of curiosity and partly because we need something. By way of introduction, I thought I would mention two qualities that I'm always looking for in people, and in the art that they make or collect or admire.

One was brought to focus for me in an article I read concerning contemporary African art. In the essay the author said he thought what distinguished contemporary African art from contemporary American and European art was a sense of urgency. I don't know whether he was right about African art, but I'm quite sure that much American and European art does lack a quality of urgency. And so, because I think the world is in trouble, I look for those who live and work with a sense of an imperative, of urgency.

The other quality for which I search in people and in art is one described by Wendell Berry in a biography of a little-known painter named Harlan Hubbard. Hubbard and his wife lived self-sufficiently by the Ohio River, and they are remembered today chiefly for their exemplary lives, though he is also known for carefully observed and deeply affectionate landscapes. After describing the pictures, Berry concludes approvingly that Hubbard was less interested in originality than in fidelity. Faithfulness.

I think that fidelity and originality are actually inseparable for an artist, because he or she must be faithful not only to the unchanging qualities in life but also to the inexhaustible newness in life, and to convey that newness requires originality. But in our time and culture, I think Berry's emphasis on the importance of fidelity is appropriate. It is all too easy to imagine a great many contemporary artists asking incredulously "fidelity to what?"

Opening statement for a discussion held at the Fraenkel Gallery, San Francisco, 2000.

ABOUT
THE HAT

WITH

WILLIAM McEWEN

WILLIAM McEWEN: First of all, congratulations on your [MacArthur] fellowship.

ROBERT ADAMS: Thank you. We're still a little dizzy from it. Though my sense of elation is qualified by the realization of how many photographers I know who have not yet been rescued— people who are doing important work and are suffering for it.

WM: Suffering—in what sense?

RA: David Smith, the sculptor, said that buyers don't pay for art— artists pay for it. He was right. Many photographers whose work we need are forced to support their picture-making by earning a living at jobs for which they are unsuited. When that happens, there's a cost. It may be that they're always tired, or don't have enough time to spend with their families, or any number of other torments.

WM: Let's talk about one of your new books, *Listening to the River*. Your other books have been collections of single images, but this is for the most part a series of sequences.

RA: The idea, as it evolved, became to suggest the experience of walking. Multiple images were a way to do this.

WM: The images in the book are verticals. Your previous pictures have tended to be horizontals.

RA: It made things interesting. As I worked I just found, some- what to my surprise, that the verticals were better pictures, so I

From Darkroom and Creative Camera Techniques *(May/June 1995). William McEwen is a fine-art photographer who specializes in portraiture; he is the author of a book of essays titled* People and Portraits.

standardized on the approach. Maybe one explanation is that the vertical orientation allowed more foreground, more of the path.

WM: Some of the sequences show the same subject in different ways.

RA: What I hoped to do was look closely, carefully. I agree with Dorothea Lange when she said that many photographers stop photographing a subject too soon, before they've exhausted its possibilities. Perhaps this is related to our traveling so much by car, surviving by glances. What I wanted to do in *Listening to the River* was to slow down and do better than survive.

WM: What equipment do you use?

RA: The photographs in *Listening to the River* were made with a 35mm Nikon F3—it's a format I'd never used for landscape before. I used just one lens throughout the project, a 28mm. It was occasionally limiting—sometimes, for example, I saw animals that I would like to have included, but couldn't because they were too far away—but limits also concentrate your vision.

WM: Do you use assistants while you're shooting?

RA: Not except while shooting the book *Summer Nights*. Chris Sublett went along with me for about six weeks, partly as an assistant and partly as a bodyguard.

WM: How about in the darkroom?

RA: No. My darkroom has been too small for more than one person. I hope to get a bigger space, though. Darkroom work is hard. Once you've made the first good print, everything afterwards is an ache. Printing for *Listening to the River*, for example, was a challenge. Over 170 images, chosen from more than 500. Some series are of five or six pictures, and were taken in as many minutes, with the sky sometimes changing and me turning this way and that. The negatives are often of various densities as a result, but I didn't want the prints to look so different as to be unrelated. So I spent a lot of time balancing things up.

WM: How much time did you spend shooting?

RA: Probably one or two percent of the time that I apply to photography as a whole—that is, shooting, developing, studying contacts, printing, exhibiting, selling work, and making books. The one or two percent in the field is of course by far the best of it. One dreams of being able to adjust the percentages around a little, though printing to order and packing and corresponding . . . running a small business . . . is very time-consuming. As is book publishing. Kerstin and I spent, for instance, hundreds of hours editing the pictures for *Listening to the River*.

WM: Did you come up with the names for each of your books?

RA: For all but one. The first book, *White Churches of the Plains*, I'd wanted to call just *White Churches*, but I lost control of the project. As near as I can determine in retrospect, the title was actually chosen, believe it or not, by the designer. She was an imperious creature! [laughs]

WM: Have you been seriously disappointed by any of your books?

RA: Not in the long run. Though in many cases there was a period of months after publication when I wasn't sure if I might have failed.

WM: What would you like to do that you haven't?

RA: Over the last two years, while I've been preparing books, I would have given a lot just to have gotten out, anywhere. No place is boring, if you've had a good night's sleep and have a pocket full of unexposed film. But to answer your question, I suppose I'd like to return to California. But I may not. The danger while photographing was sufficient to raise some questions. Kerstin is against my working there again.

WM: What do you mean by "danger"?

RA: It was a landscape with a lot of anger in it. In the chaparral, particularly, there was evidence of people you didn't want to meet—lots of junk and the sounds of dirt bikes and assault weapons. And even in many neighborhoods, if that's what they should be called, there was a feeling of intense hostility . . . razor wire, and house after house with aggressive dogs—pit bulls, Rottweilers, Dobermans. One had to be extremely alert.

WM: You've used the word *art* frequently in discussing photography. Why?

RA: I think the word has, when considered historically, a meaning. Not a narrow or simple definition, but a definition nonetheless, and a useful one. But many—not just those in photography—have either abandoned the word or tried to co-opt it, often for commercial reasons. The result has been costly, both to society in general and to artists in particular. The confusion—the laziness—has contributed, for example, to the downward spiral at the National Endowment for the Arts. Few people will venture now to try to say, even in the broadest terms, what art is, and thus there is no way to set standards for success. If everything a so-called artist makes is art, then, as some wit has observed, pencils don't need erasers and toilets don't need to flush. Our unwillingness to try to define what we're about has given Jesse Helms and others like him a fat target.

WM: What is art, then?

RA: Basically, it's an attempt, by fond attention to the world, to find redeeming metaphor in it. Ultimately art's gift to us is the pleasurable implication of coherence, of meaning, of consequence. I tried to write about this in a little book called *Beauty in Photography*, and more recently in a collection of essays titled *Why People Photograph*.

WM: Your published writings tend to stick to the subject of photography. Do you use the pen to try to understand what you do with the camera?

RA: Thinking is talking to yourself, and writing things down can sometimes help clarify the muddle.

WM: You once wrote that there are too many photographers.

RA: Did I say that? Maybe I meant that there are too many people who need to make a living by it. I don't really believe you can have too many good photographers. It's like writing. There can't be too much good writing.

WM: You spent some time on Michigan's Upper Peninsula when you were younger. Have you considered returning there?

RA: Yes. One of the places Kerstin and I would like to see again is Eagle Harbor. We'd like to go back. But not in the winter!

WM: Will you make photographs there?

RA: I hadn't really thought about it. I have to be in a place a little while before I want to work. If I just arrive and start shooting, it isn't quite right.

WM: Why don't you go to places like Yosemite to make pictures?

RA: In general, places like Yosemite make me sad. It's the crowding.

WM: With all of the pictures and all of the books, what are you trying to accomplish in your life of photography?

RA: I suppose to learn how not to complain. Robert Frost said that the best achievement in life is to learn to be good-natured. That sounds pretty close. And very hard. I'm like that woman who took her little boy to the beach and saw a wave wash him out to sea. She promised God that if He'd return her child she'd never ask for anything else, and the next wave deposited the boy safely back on the shore. She ran and hugged him, but then noticed that he'd lost his cap. "The hat, Lord," she demanded. "What about the hat?"

WM: You've always struck me as being good-natured, so apparently you've succeeded.

RA: For the odd millisecond! [laughs] Some of the best times are when I'm photographing. It helps me forget the hat. It helps me to pay attention to the beauty of what has been given. Photographers, unlike philosophers, tend to focus on what's there rather than what isn't.

ALONG
SOME RIVERS

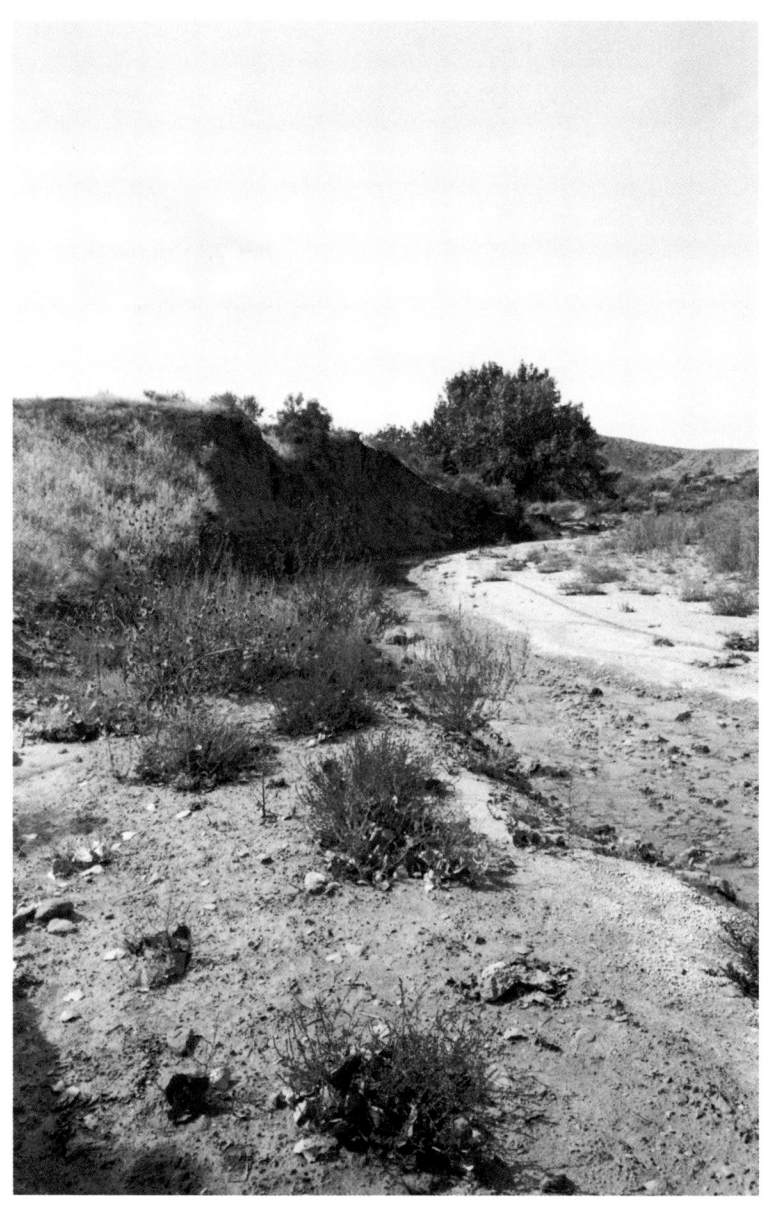

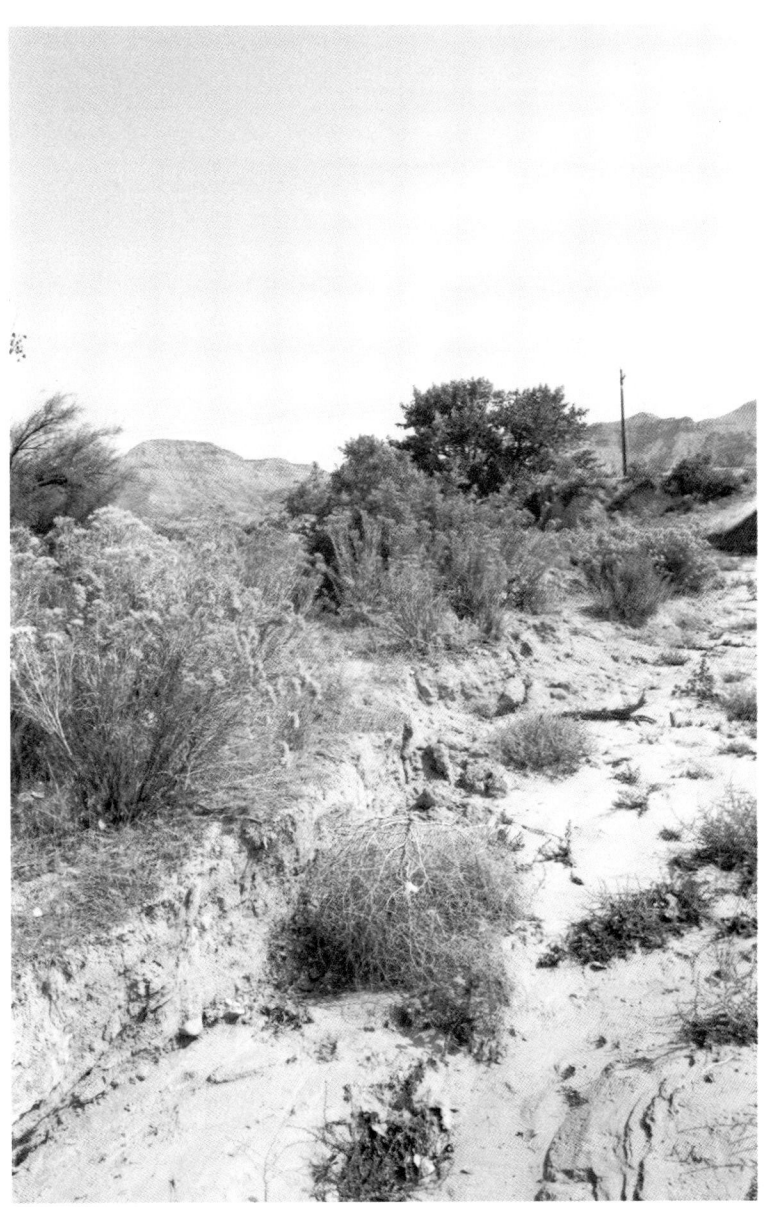

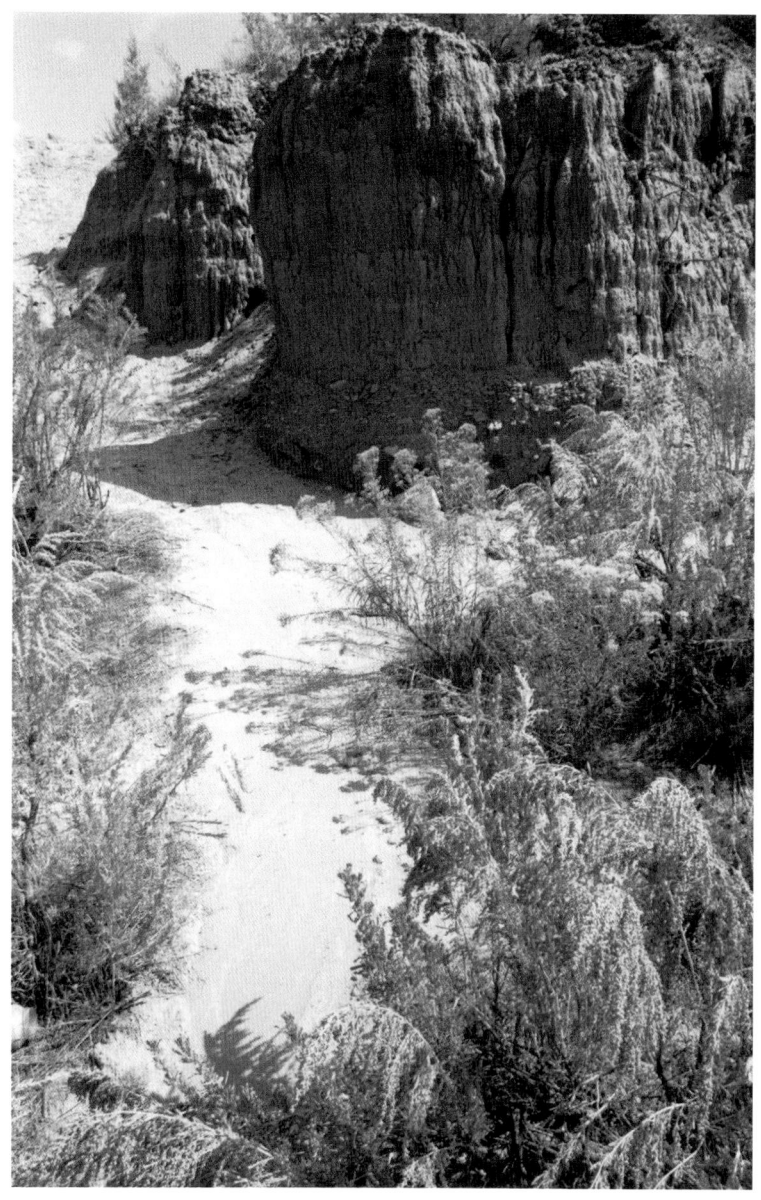

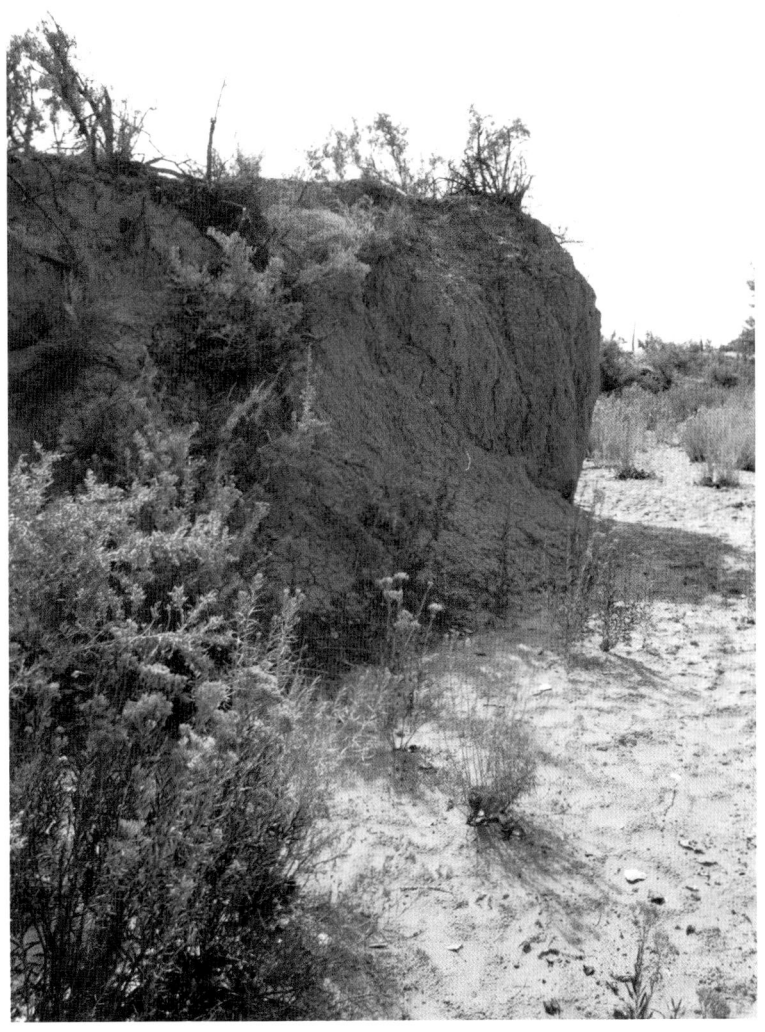

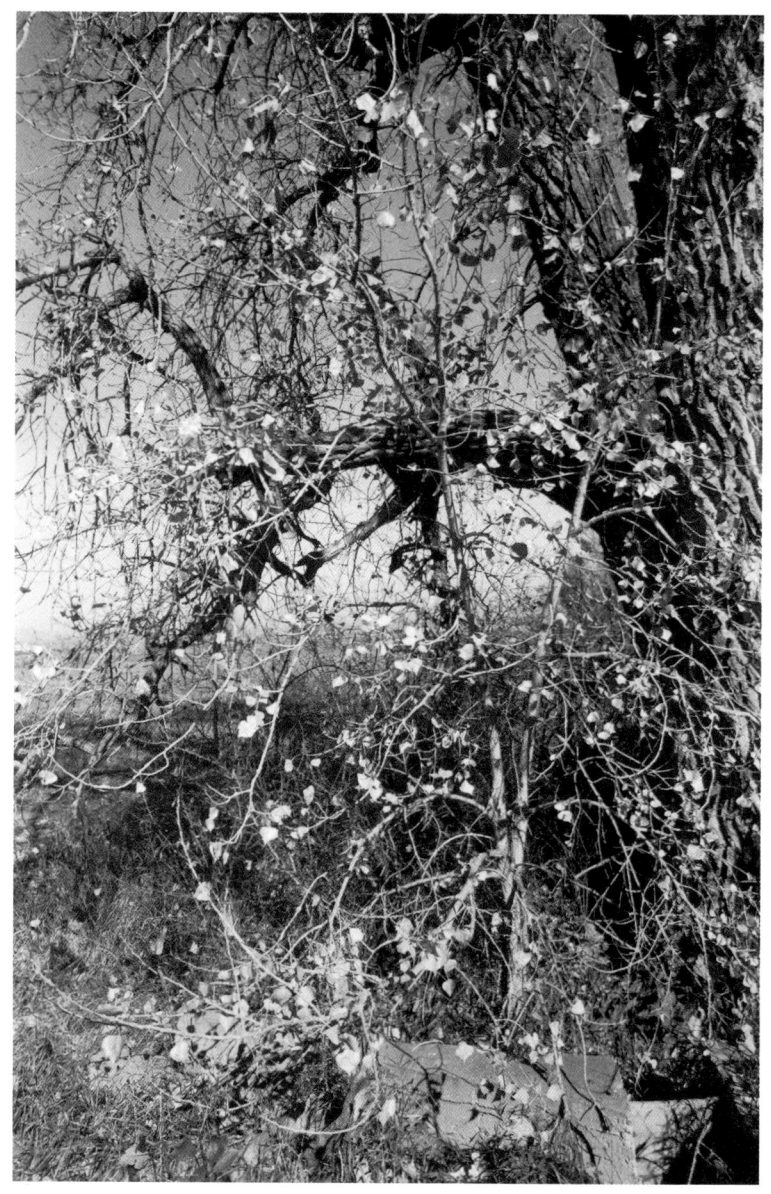

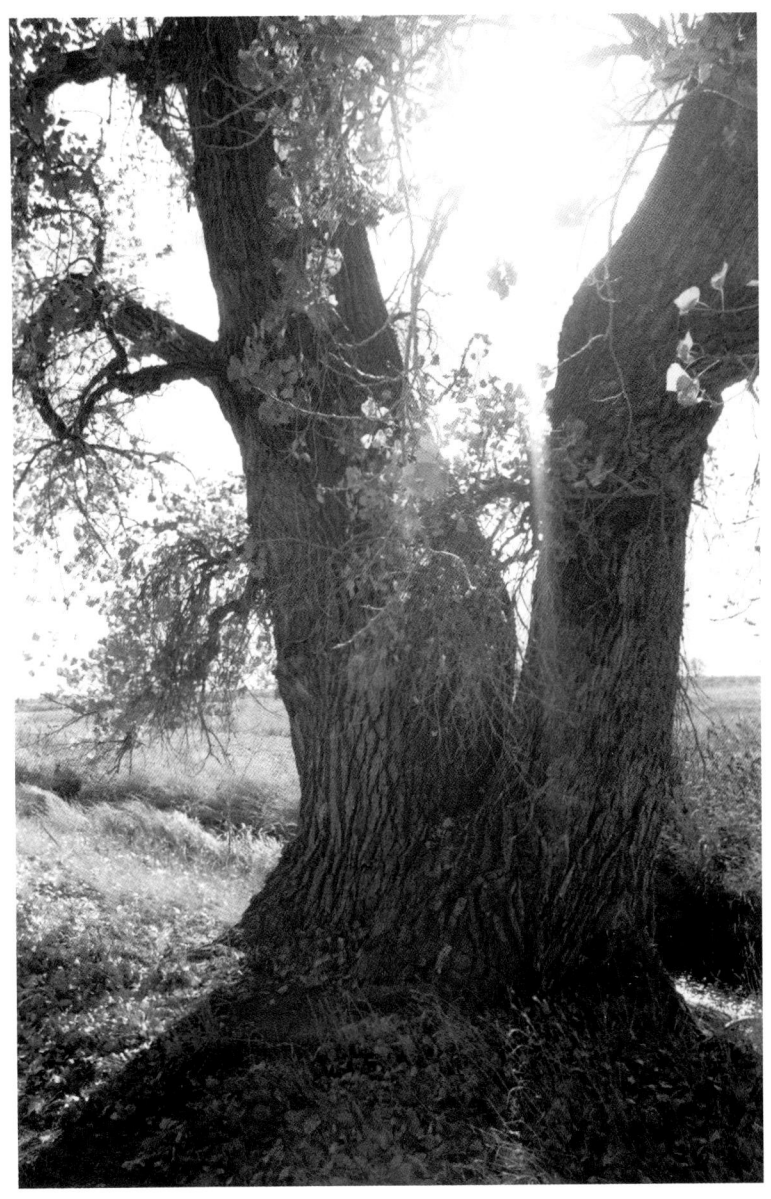

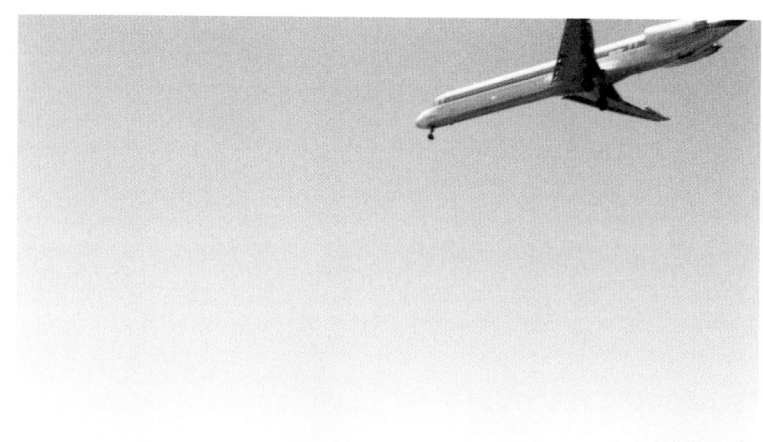

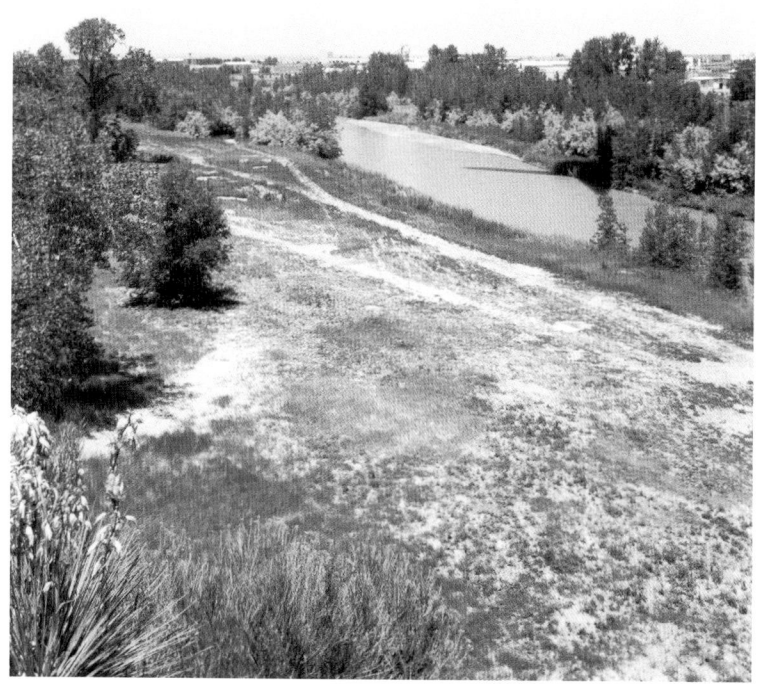

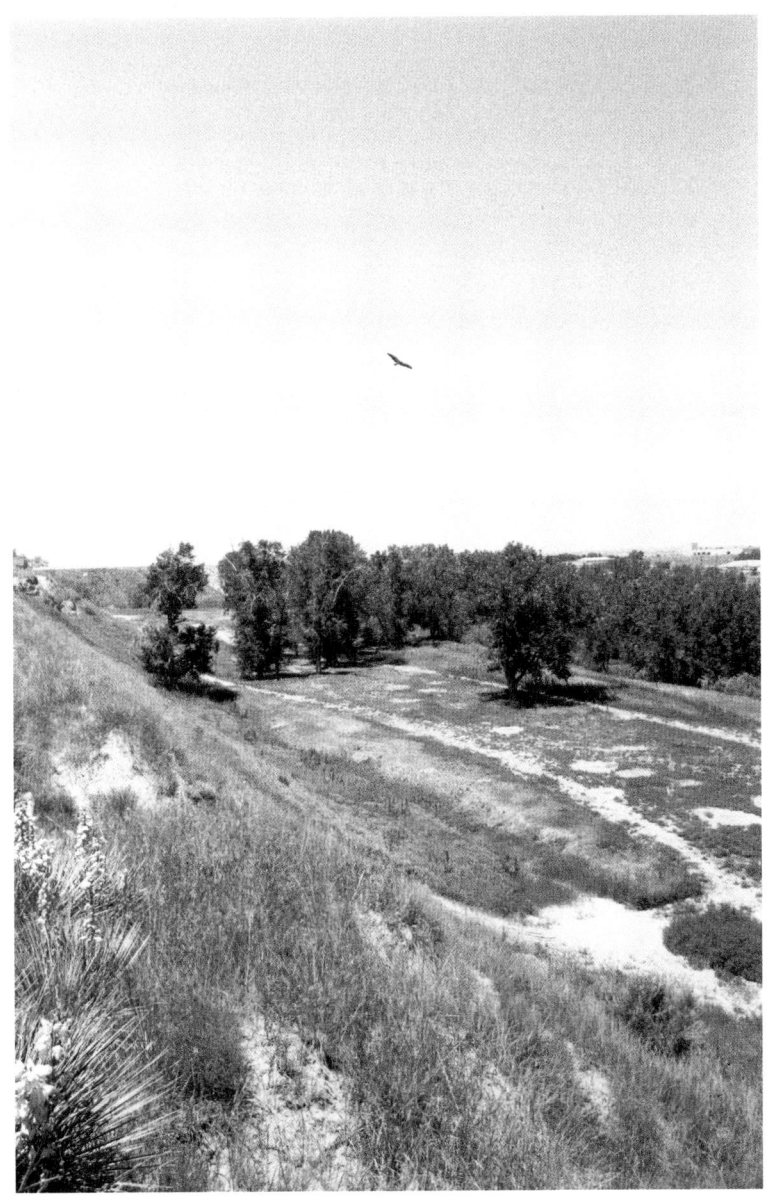

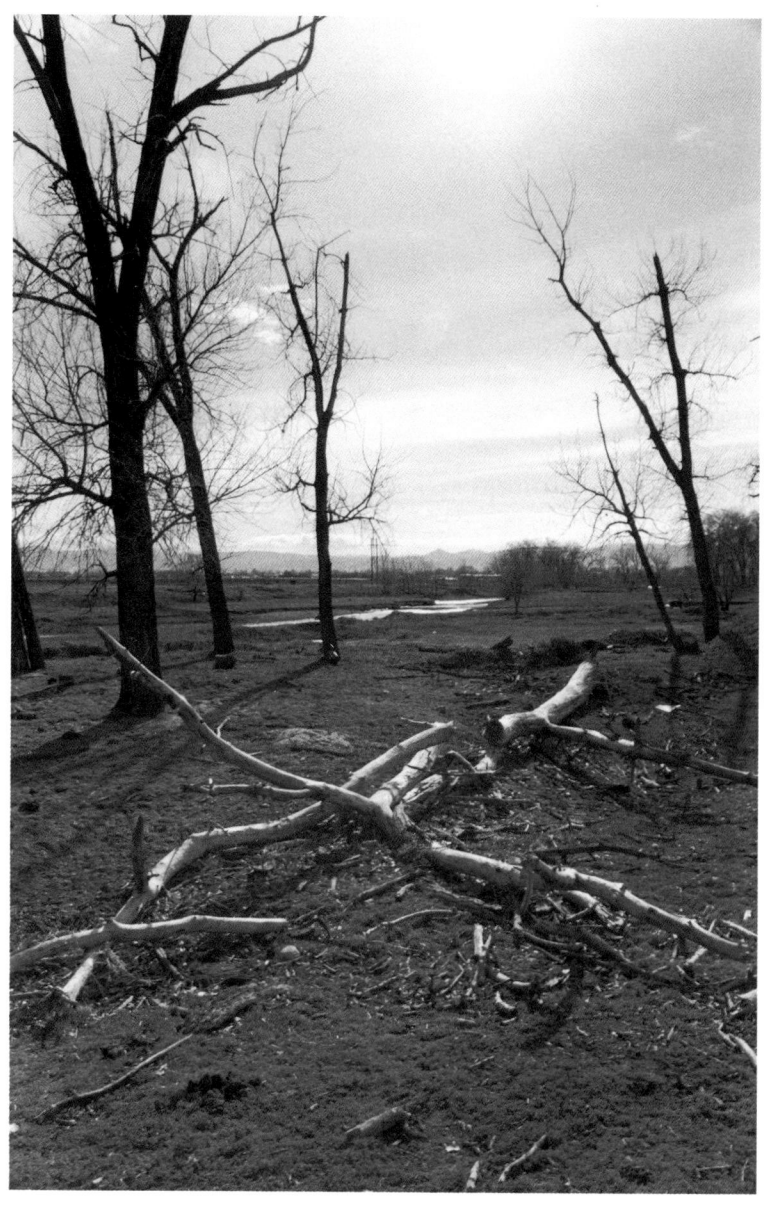

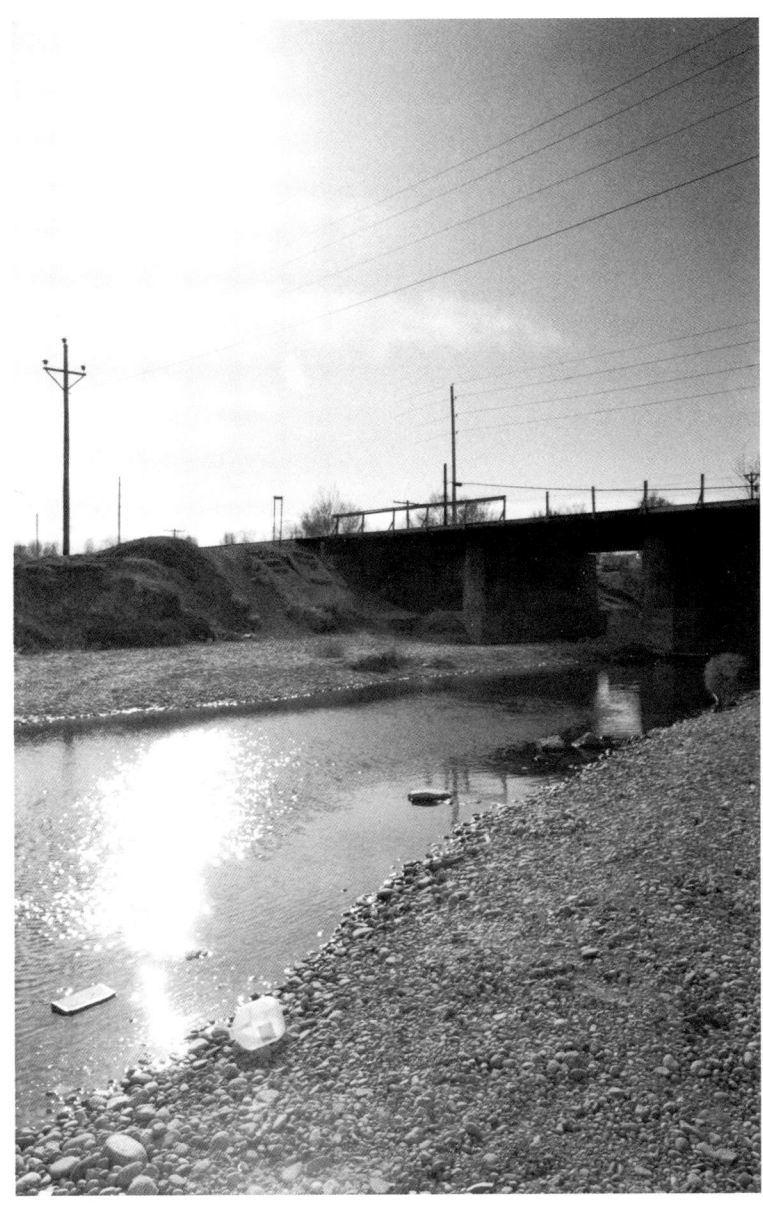

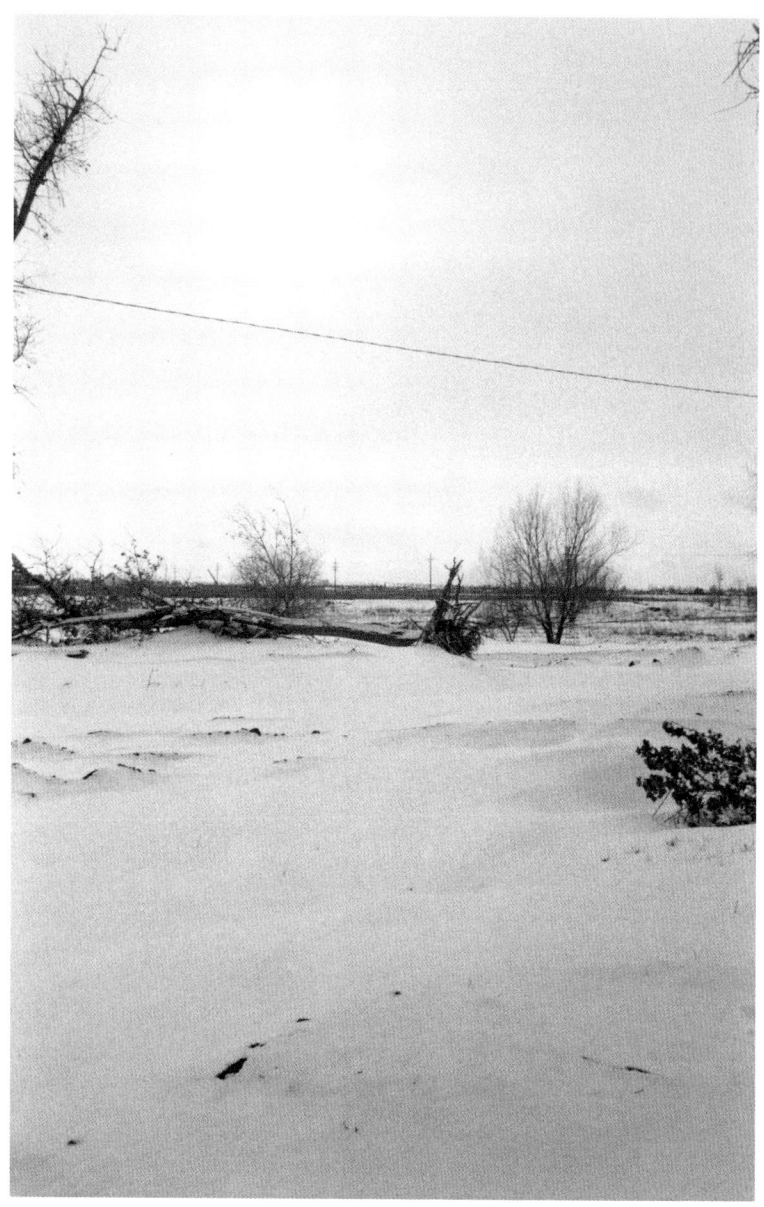

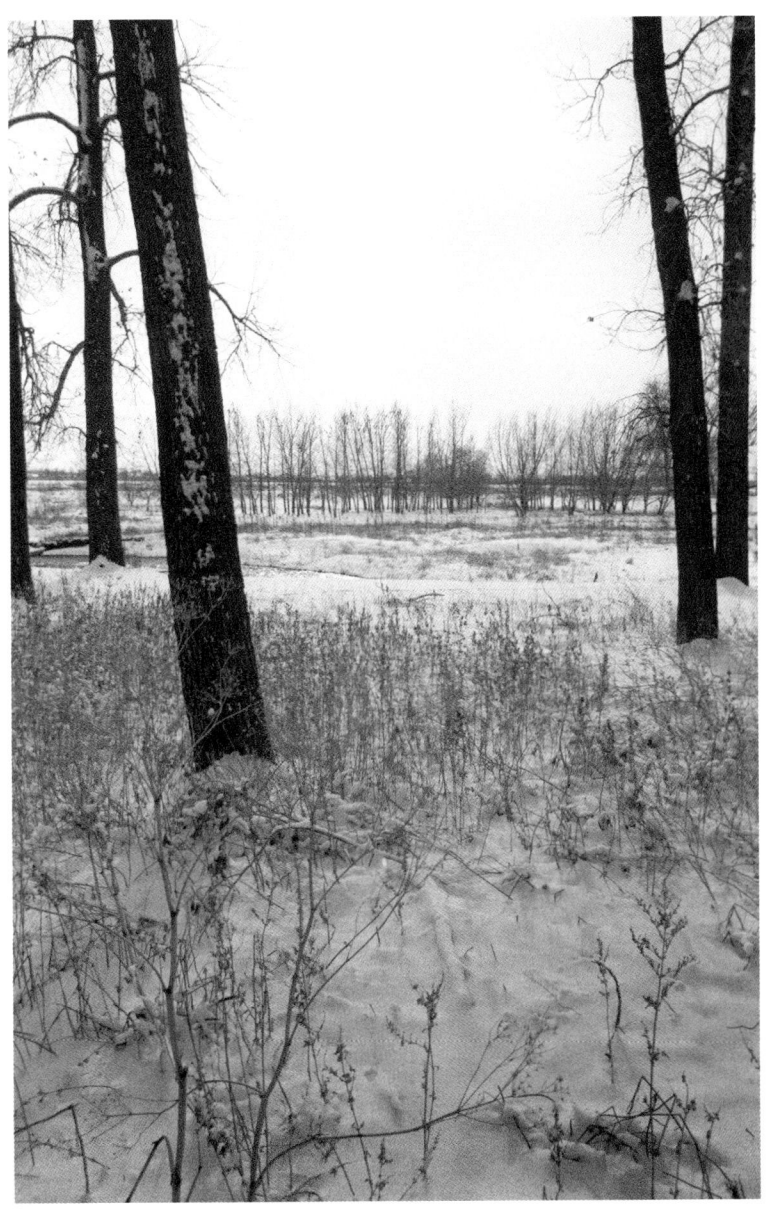

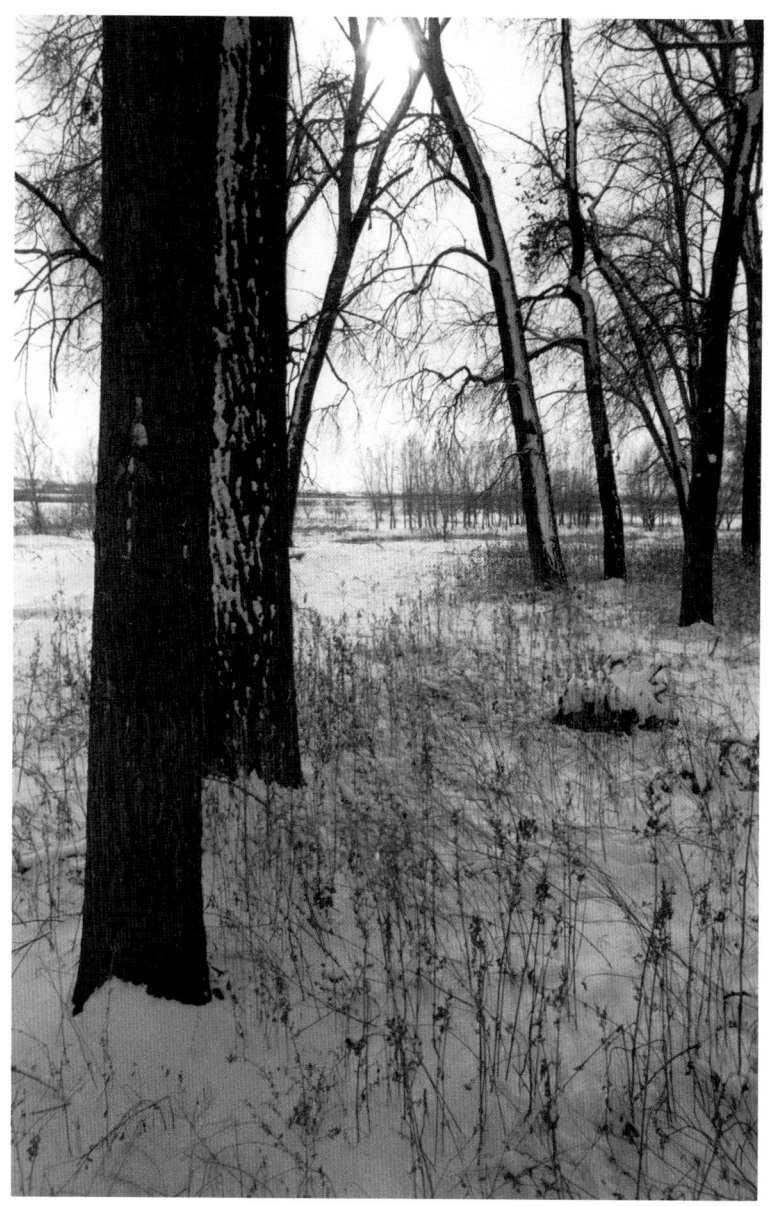

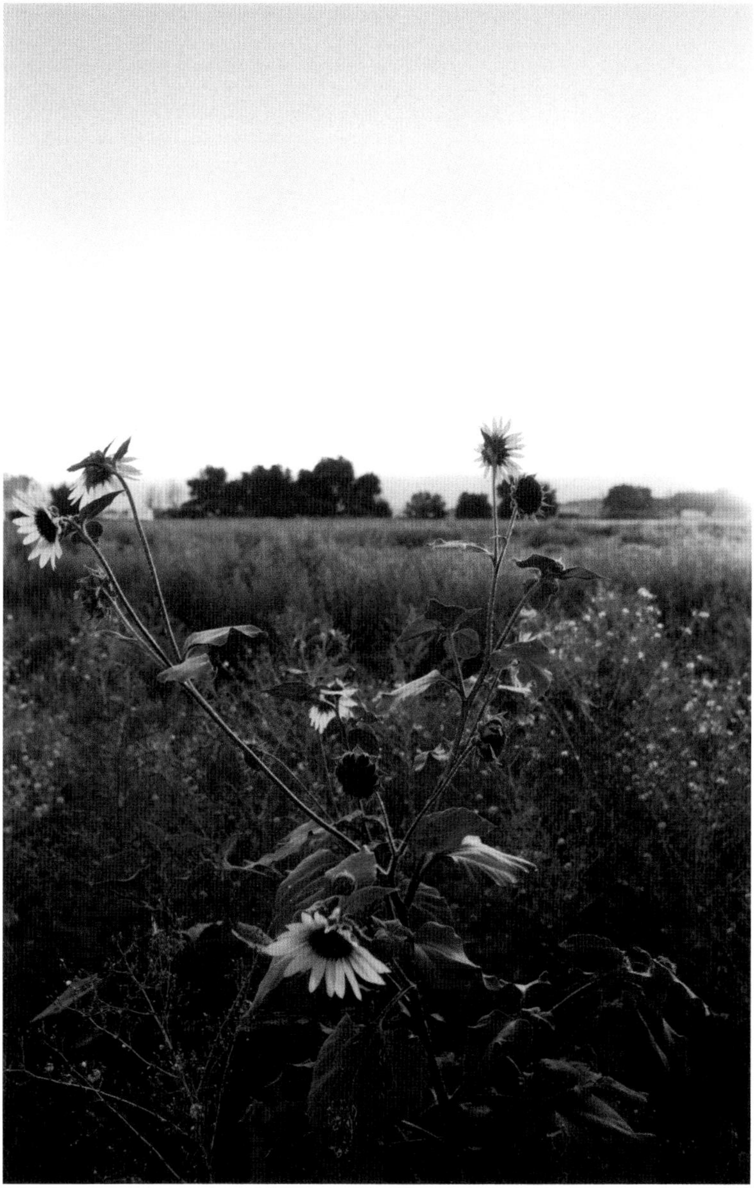

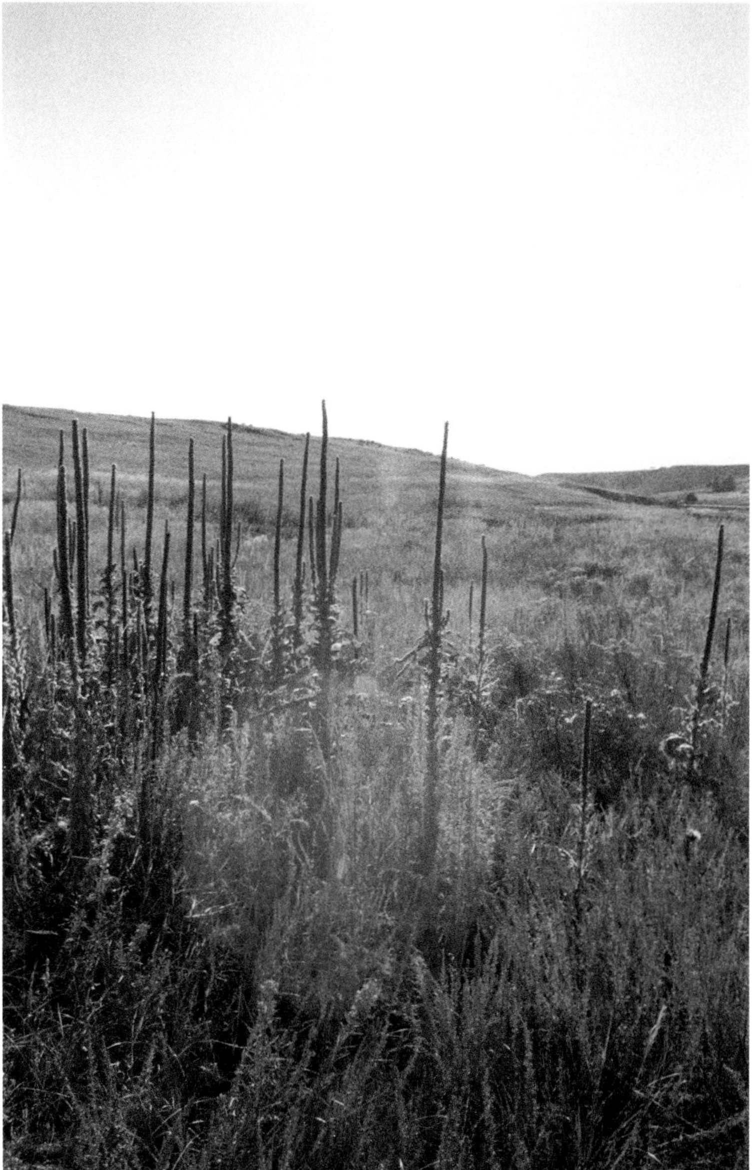

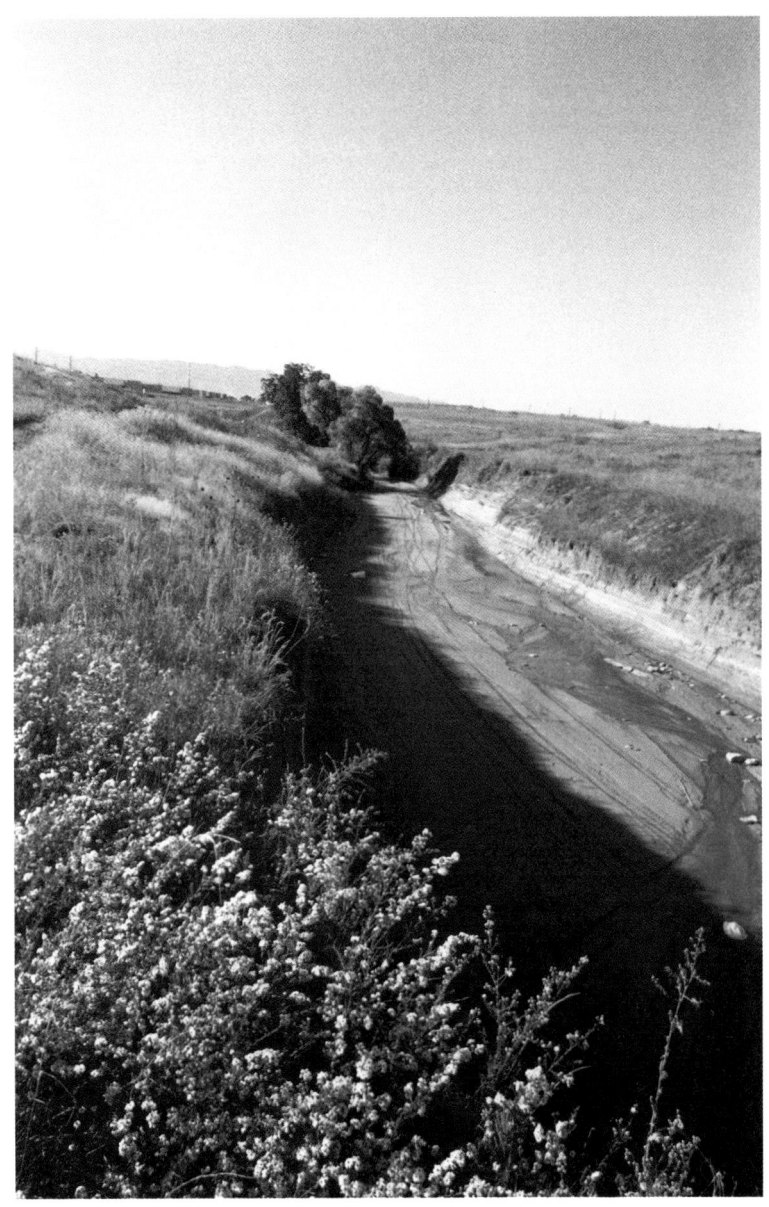

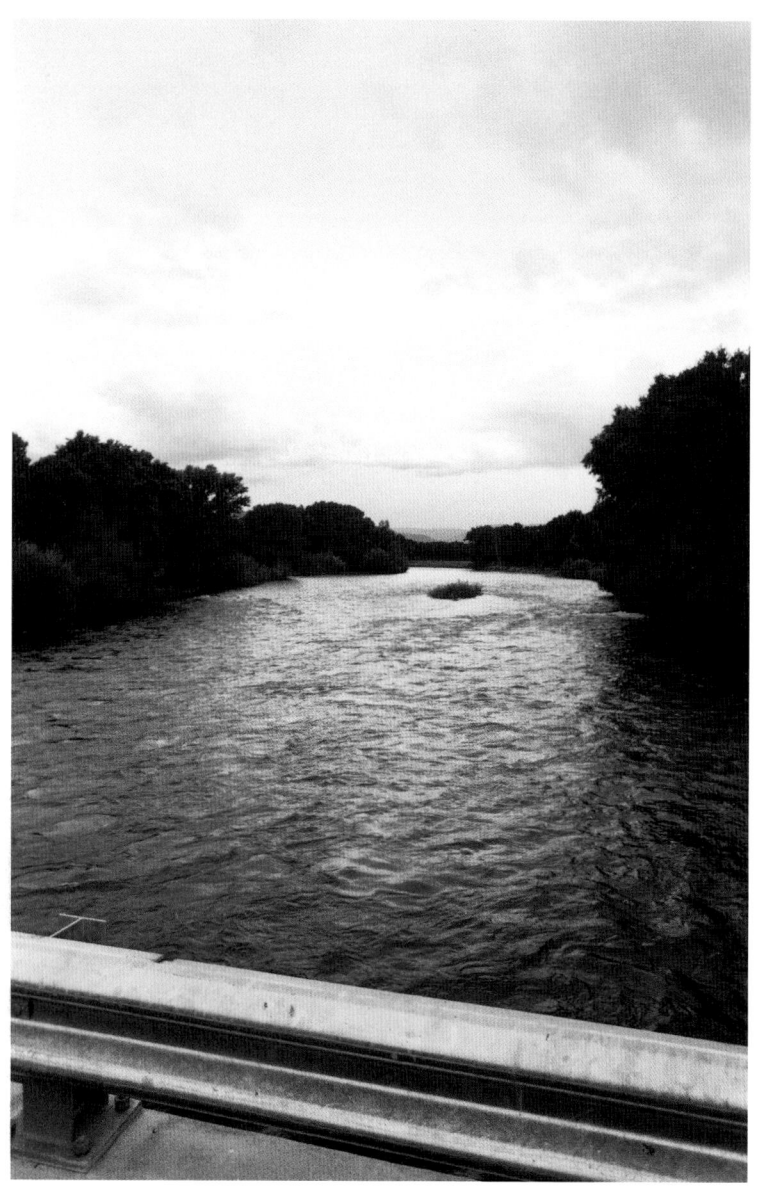

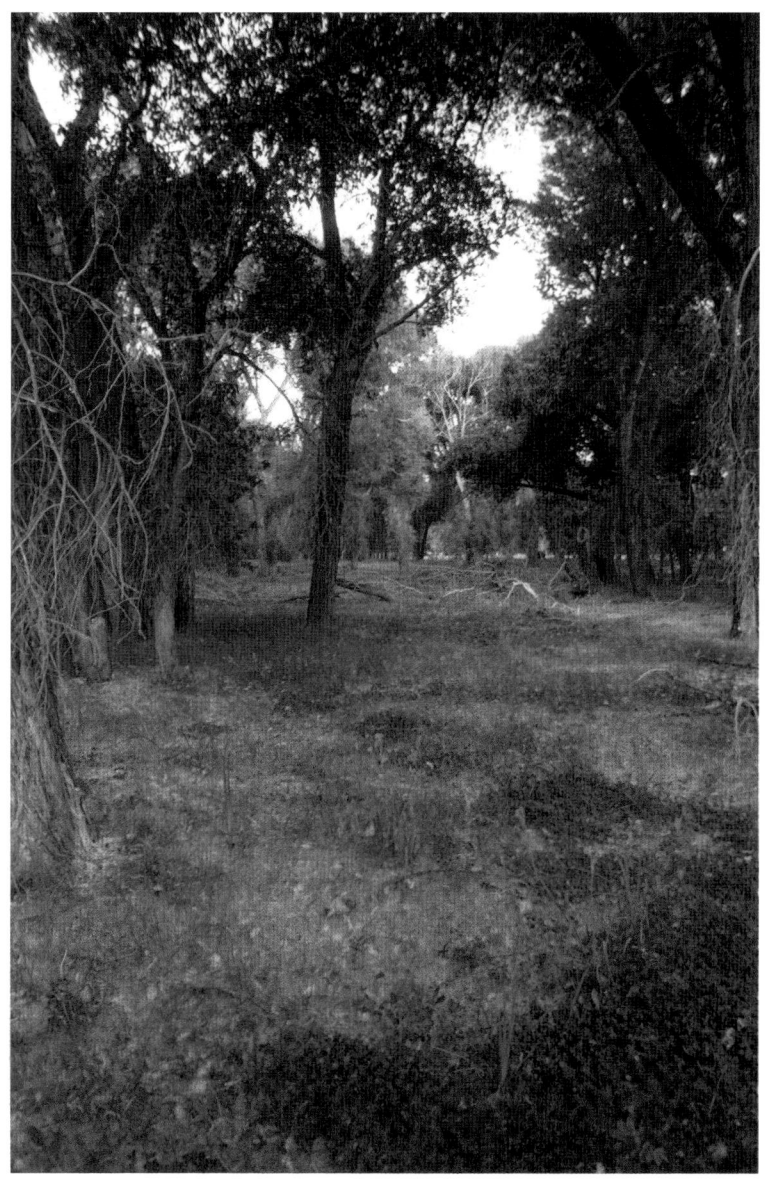

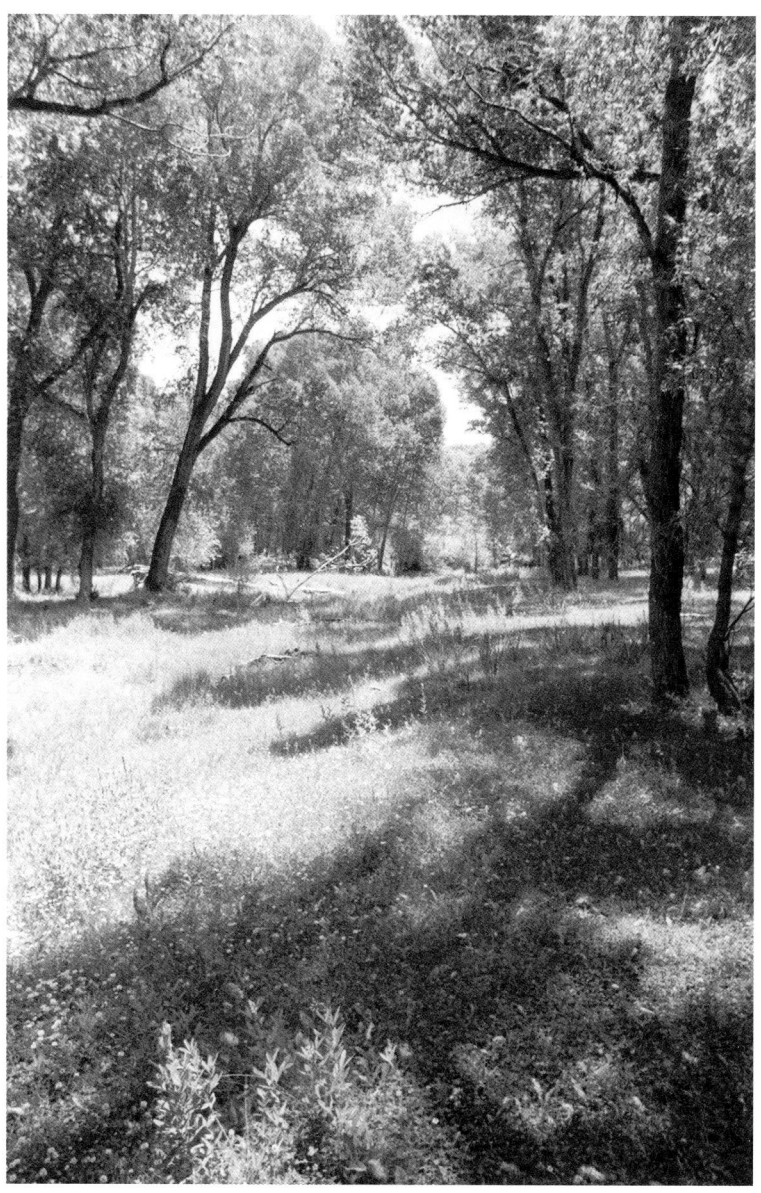

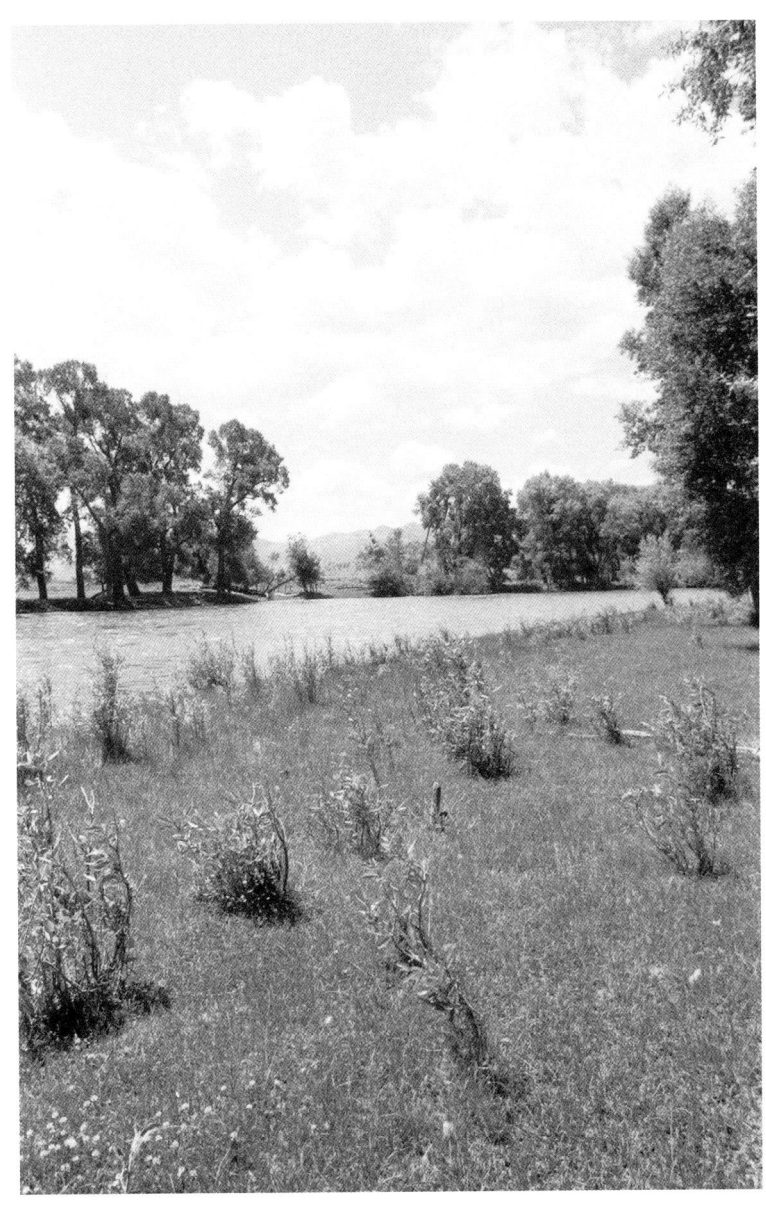

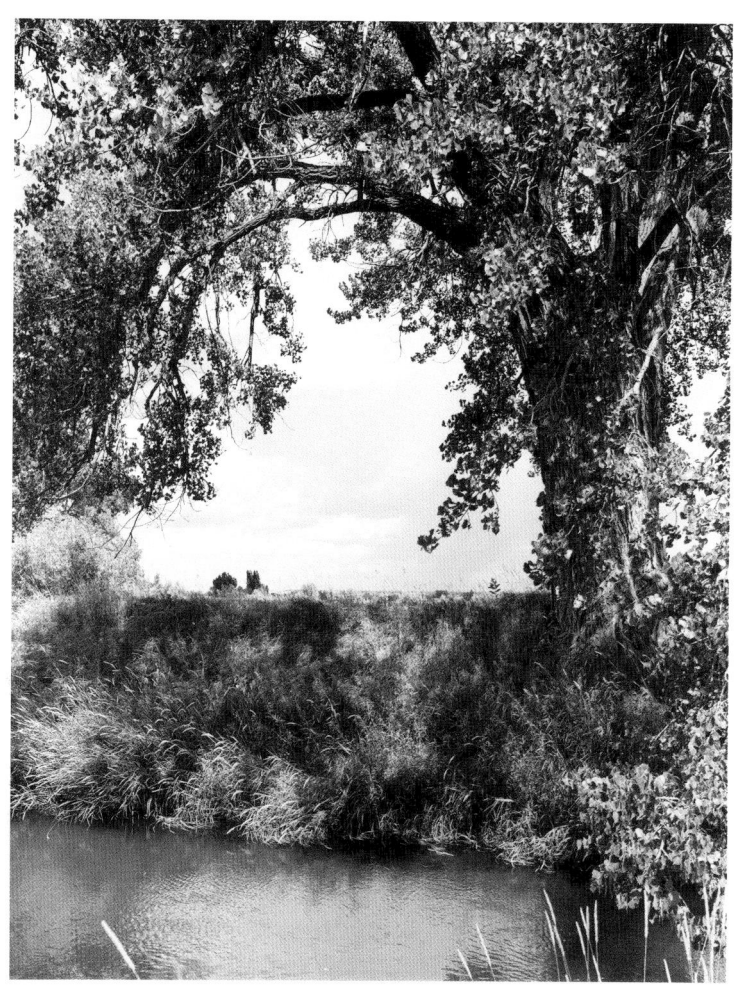

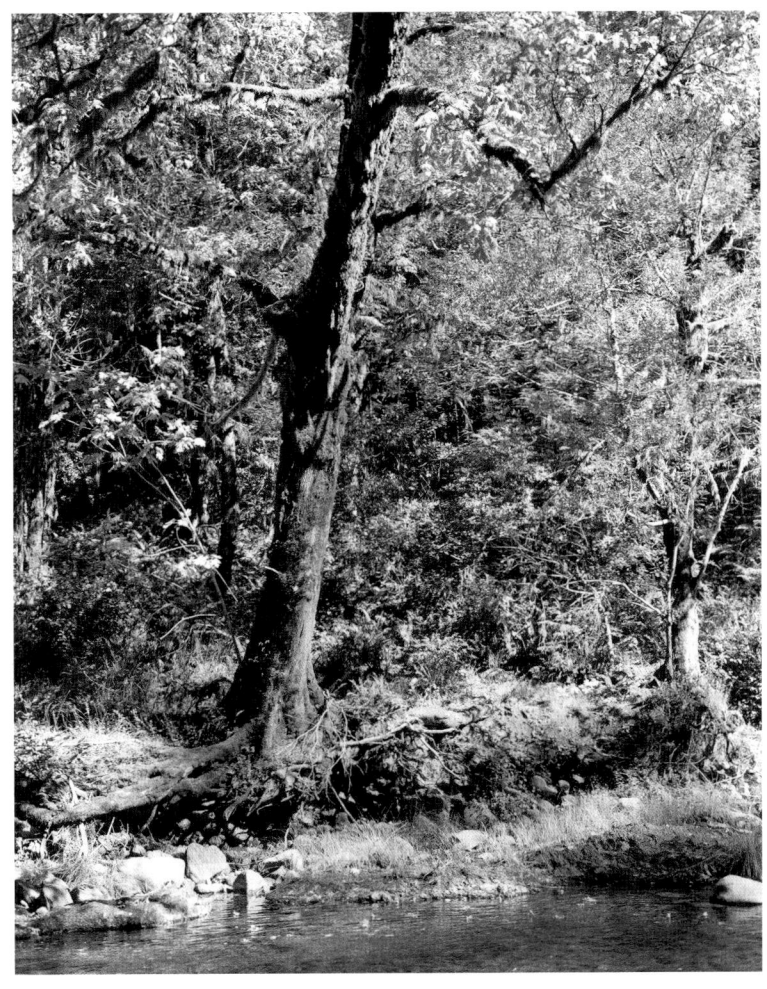

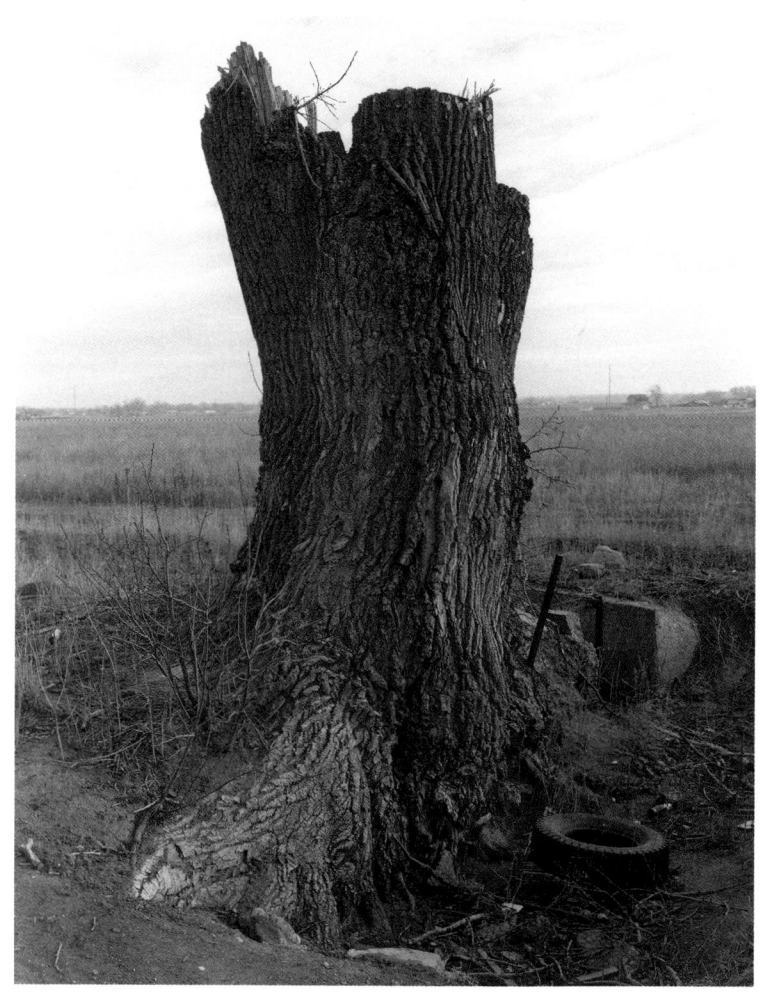

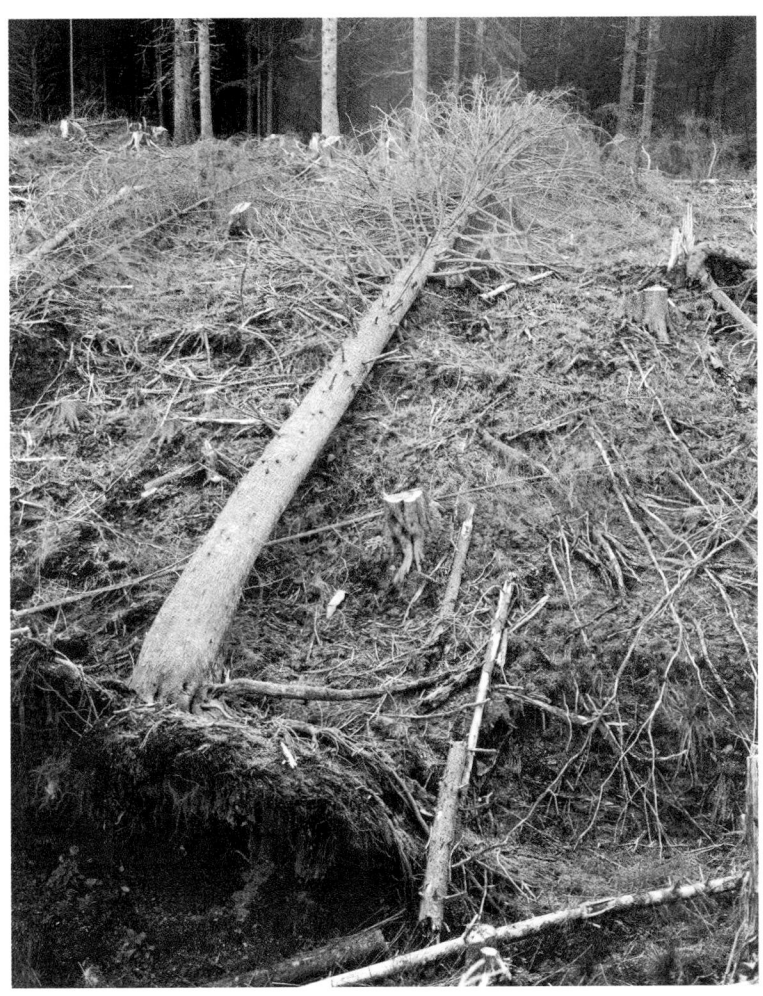

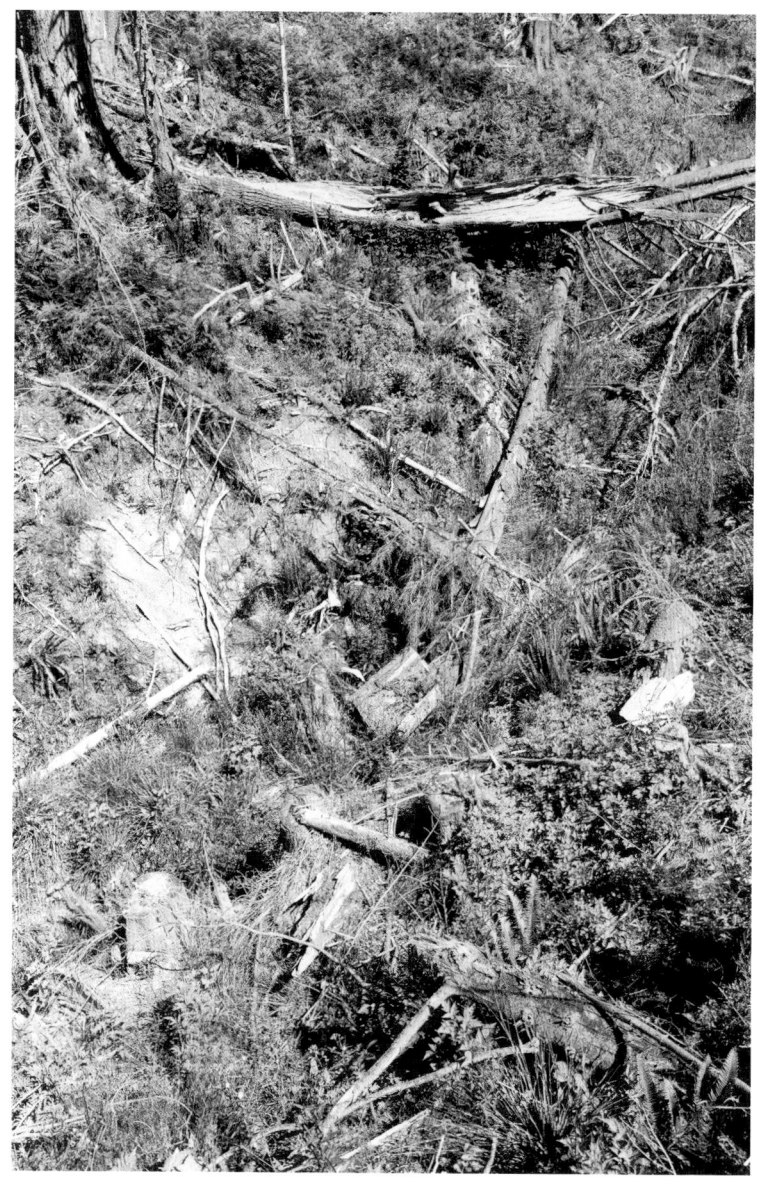

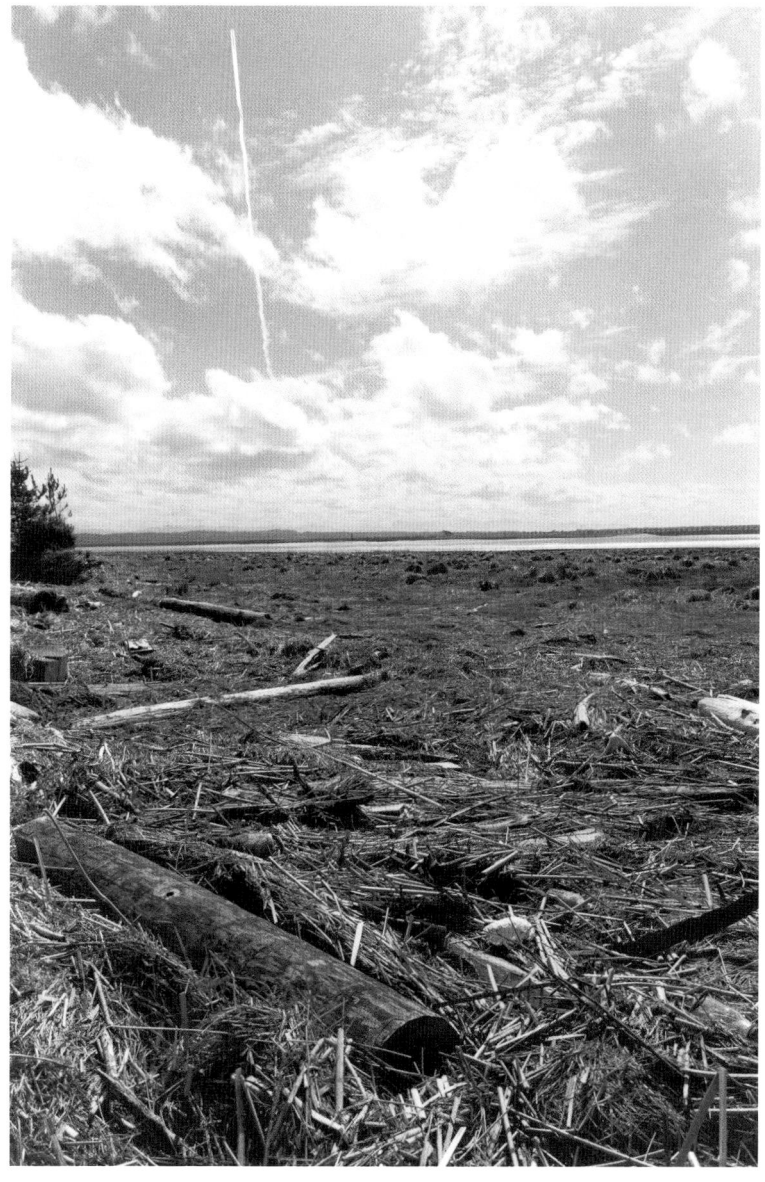

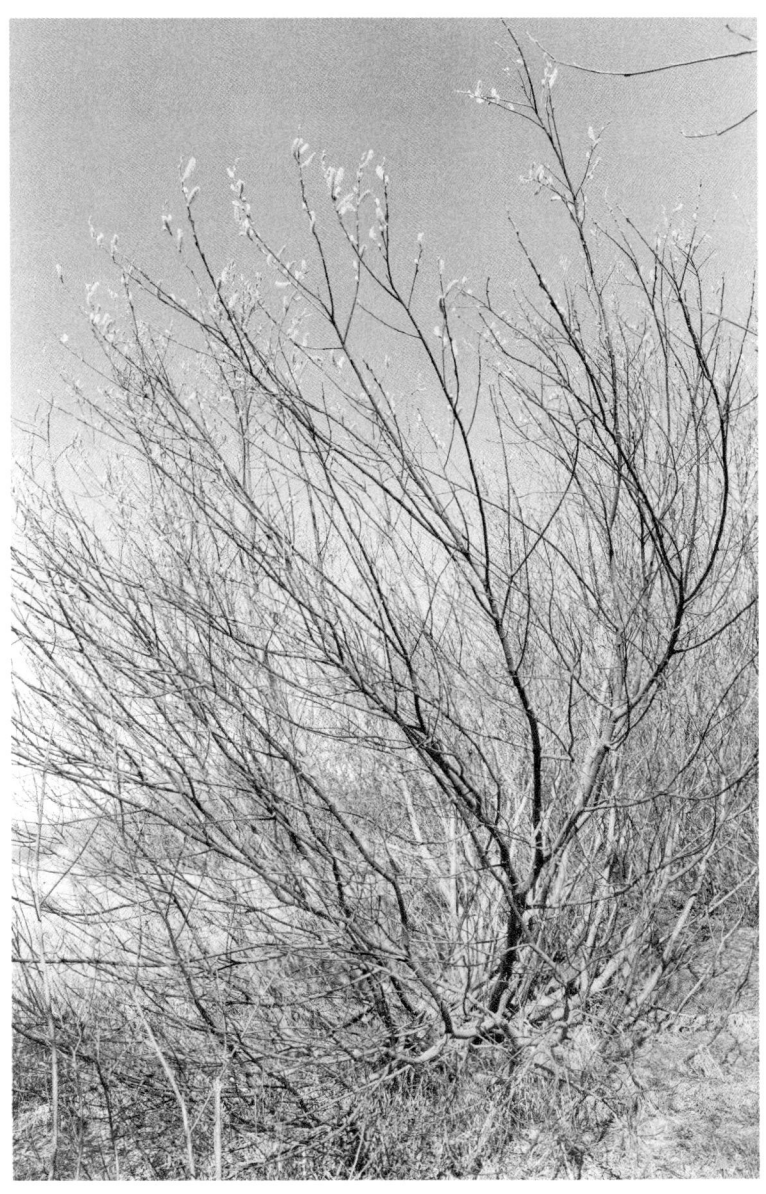

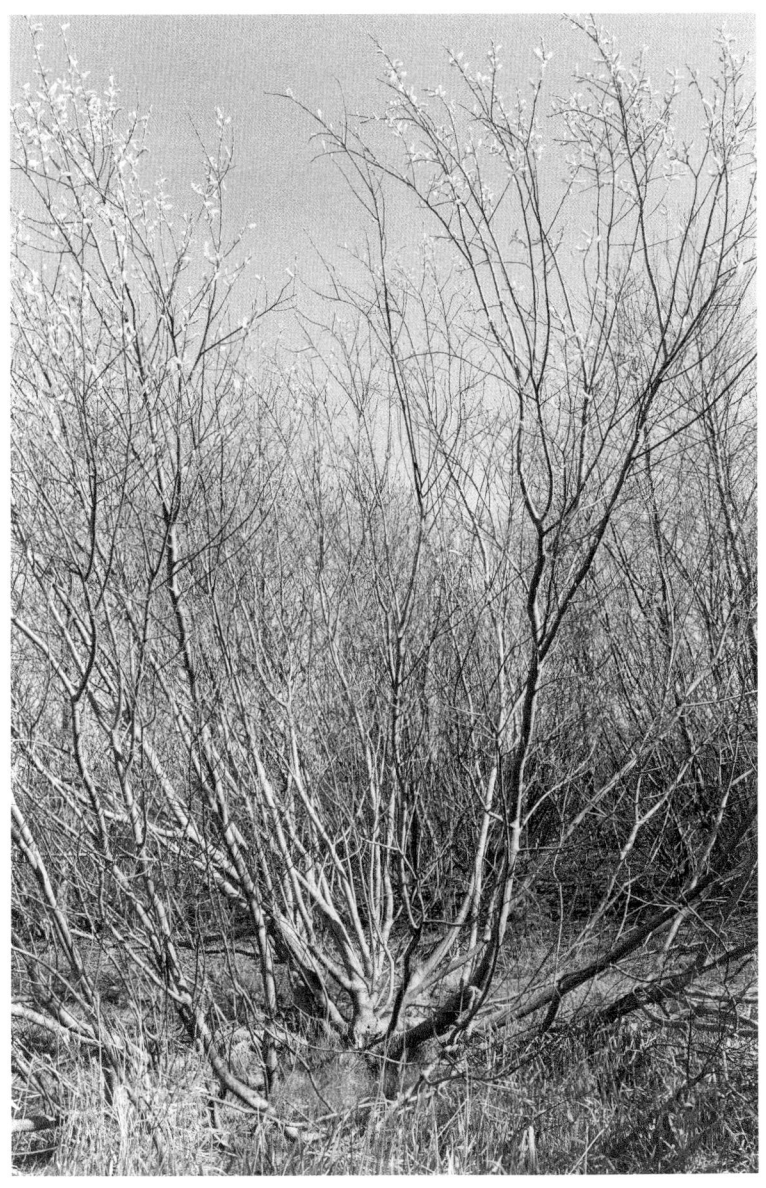

PLATES

ABOUT
THE NEW WEST

WITH

THOMAS WESKI

THOMAS WESKI: What are your impressions when you look back at *The New West* now (it was first published in 1974)?

ROBERT ADAMS: I am struck again by how beautiful the landscape was, in spite of everything. And I can't help thinking how much more disaster there was to come.

TW: What is the region like today?

RA: Overpopulation and corporate capitalism have accelerated and broadened the failures that were developing at the time of the book.

TW: What led you to take the pictures?

RA: Pleasure. The light was compelling. I remember once, at the end of a long summer day of picture-taking, I found myself so exhausted from trying to record the last light over the suburbs that I couldn't work the camera. When would the light ever be that way again, I thought.

TW: Are you continuing to photograph?

RA: I just finished developing ninety rolls.

TW: What keeps you working?

RA: Frank Dobie, the Texas historian, said it: "The wildflowers of a rainy spring and the grasses of a showery summer are good and beautiful and sufficient even though they vanish."

From the second edition of The New West *(Cologne: Walter König, 2000).*

69

ABOUT
TURNING BACK
STUDENTS FROM REED COLLEGE

STUDENT: I'm a freshman. I try to paint. But I can't really paint, because I can't seem to push my work beyond things that are just beautiful. They seem superficial, without any conceptual backup.

ROBERT ADAMS: It's your first year. After you suffer some more . . . [laughter]

STUDENT: I like light. I like water. I like the way the sunset looks on my wall in my dorm.

RA: Perfect!

STUDENT: But it's sort of . . .

RA: You know, eventually the light on the wall is going to pick up something that isn't quite what you expected. Then you're in business.

STUDENT: I like art with intellectual complexity.

RA: So do I, in some respects. But it's easy to confuse philosophy and art. They're not the same. It's an easy distinction to forget in school—particularly a good school like Reed, where you're urged to live an active life of the mind. A great picture is a *concretized* universal. The strength of that is that it can and has to be cross-referenced out to life in the street. Philosophy carries within itself no such test. "Conceptual art" seems to me, not surprisingly, an irreconcilable contradiction in terms.

■ ■ ■

From a conversation held in Astoria, Oregon, at an old cannery next to the Columbia River, March 2001. The book Turning Back: A Photographic Journal of Re-exploration *(Fraenkel Gallery and Matthew Marks Gallery, 2005), which takes the occasion of the Lewis and Clark bicentennial to document the condition of Northwestern forests, was in preparation at the time.*

RA: Art history has an appalling pedigree. It comes out of nineteenth-century German philosophy. I don't know if it's ever going to recover. [laughter]

∎ ∎ ∎

RA: Art has traditionally recognized two obligations: to tell the truth and to affirm the truth. The problem currently is that many artists are saying no, that isn't my job—I can't do that, and won't try. And so they in turn are largely ignored, or held up in the press as jokes. And why not? Who needs more nihilism? Anyone can arrive there without help.

The challenge for artists is just as it is for everyone: to face facts and somehow come up with a *yes*, to try for alchemy. No wonder the instances of artistic success are costly and rare and impure. And deeply loved. And utterly out of the reach of most journalists.

Today is Van Gogh's birthday. Think about the cost. Here was a person who didn't live beyond his thirties, and yet look how we value his achievement. It was bought with blood. His life is an example both of failure and of success. There are many of his pictures that make me extremely uncomfortable, because they don't go beyond anxiety. But some reach the goal, which is peace.

∎ ∎ ∎

LEO RUBINFIEN: You've often said that you think things went to hell starting with Marcel Duchamp. I wonder if you would talk about why.

RA: My feeling is that Duchamp has not been a helpful guide. His argument seems to have been the one offered in Vietnam—we need to destroy the village in order to save it, we need to destroy art in order to save art. But at the end of the day, what we have is just a urinal. . . .

∎ ∎ ∎

RA: A photographer's power consisted, before digitization, in the capacity to determine what's in, what's out, what's in focus, what the tonal range will be. . . . You've got many ways to craft shape, you just don't have a painter's tools, which allow you to start from scratch.

STUDENT: But you would still use your imagination.

RA: Yes, though I suppose, being a classicist, I like the art that denies itself the most, that uses the most rigorously limited means and still manages to get there. George Steiner defined classicism as "art by privation," and that does seem to me to be the most powerful kind. Usually. Although one says something like that, and immediately somebody comes up with an utterly convincing exception. [laughter]

So far, most of what I've seen that's been digitally reworked has something wrong with it. Something betrays it. There's often something fishy about the light. But it is possible digitally to alter things and come up with convincing pictures; witness those by Andreas Gursky. Although I have to add that the process strikes me as a tool, not a new key to the meaning of life. The old questions remain. Aeschylus and Sophocles and Shakespeare are not made irrelevant by new technology.

※ ※ ※

RA: When I'm photographing in clear-cuts, I know that what has brought me there is a sense of the world coming apart. But after I've been there long enough to get over my shock at the violence, after I've been working an hour or two and am absorbed in the structure of things as they appear in the finder, I'm not thinking only about the disaster. I'm discovering things in sunlight. You can stand in the most hopeless place and if it's in daylight you can experience moments that are right, that are whole.

That's not to say that working in clear-cuts has been easy. So much effort has had to go to trying *not* to do certain things. *Not* to use the sky, on those rare occasions when there is one here in the Northwest, to rescue the land. *Not* to be seduced into celebrating the power of men and machines, which can have a Satanic beauty and heroism about it. And *not* to aestheticize the carnage.

■ ■ ■

RA: The observance in 2005 of the Lewis and Clark bicentennial ought not to be about discovering the West—that's over—but rediscovering the East. It was in the going back that the Corps of Discovery managed to foul up; it was then that they killed Indians and made some pointlessly dangerous forays, and of course Lewis ended up an apparent suicide. We need to do better than they did on the return trip. Maya Lin has been commissioned to produce monuments along the Lewis and Clark route in Idaho and Washington, and I suggested to her husband, Daniel Wolf, whom I know a little, that the monument at the mouth of the Columbia ought to be located not only for a view of the Pacific but a view back upriver. Eastward. That's the frontier, and it's dangerous.

■ ■ ■

STUDENT: Have you ever been attacked while you were photographing?

RA: No. Once or twice people have been very angry. I have some sympathy with their anger. This is a society where we're all afraid a lot of the time. I do try my best never to print pictures of people that are defamatory. Unless they deserve it. [laughter] Of course, you can make mistakes. When I took pictures of people on the street for *Our Lives and Our Children*, I was very uncomfortable doing it. I'm sure there were times when I took pictures when, if I'd known that person's story, I wouldn't have done it.

STUDENT: Your own anger seems directed at the lower classes.

RA: I have a hard time with the mass-produced junk that they sometimes uncritically accept. But my real quarrel is with a system that so maldistributes wealth that a majority remains uneducated. I think that's why our democracy is going to fail.

※ ※ ※

RA: One of the great things about Dorothea Lange is that at her best she did not see in terms of stereotypes. She saw in terms of individuals, even though she was also concerned with large social issues. That seems to me the balance that is needed. Sad to say, many stereotypes have a grain of truth in them (the social sciences focus on that grain of truth, which is what makes them so corrosive to the spirit).

※ ※ ※

STUDENT: Was art important to you growing up?

RA: Not as we've been defining it. My parents' training was in mathematics and speech pathology. I remember only one picture on the walls of our house.

Their gifts to me were of other sorts. There is a passage in Hemingway's "Fathers and Sons," for example, that has always meant a lot to me: "His father was with him, suddenly, in deserted orchards and in new-plowed fields, in thickets, on small hills, or when going through dead grass, whenever splitting wood or hauling water, by grist mills, cider mills and dams and always with open fires."

※ ※ ※

RA: Here's a heresy for you: I think Dorothea Lange was greater than Walker Evans.

STUDENT: There's a lot of criticism of Dorothea Lange for being a sentimentalist.

RA: You have to say what you mean by the word. For many people, *any* emotional response is inappropriate. [laughter] It's the age of cool. But the most perfect expression of coolness is being dead.

Lange, it seems to me, was brave in her record of human suffering. She didn't turn away. Look at the portrait of the president of the Southern Tenant Farmers' Union. Look at the man's eyes. He knows he's not going to win.

But she knew there were aspects of life to enjoy, too. Shortly before her death, for example, she published a small book of pictures that she made of her family at a cabin on the shore near San Francisco. I often turn to that book when I'm tired. I thank her for it—for its warmth.

ABOUT
CONTINUING
WITH

PETER BROWN

PETER BROWN: You are both a photographer and a writer, and while the photographic side has obviously held precedence for you, I'm interested in the ways that you've dealt with these two abilities over the years. How has each influenced the other?

ROBERT ADAMS: I'm only a writer a little bit. As Fran Lebowitz said (I love it!): "I write so slowly I could write with my own blood and not hurt myself."

The puzzle is not only to figure out what one might have the gift and skill to say, but to figure out what can only be said and what can only be shown. A still photograph, for example, rarely by itself does justice to complex moral issues, whereas a book of essays might. Though essays rarely do justice to a tree, whereas a photograph might.

There aren't any rules, just the final test of whether a specific piece of writing or picture-making is effective. Assuming that the main challenge of life is to love life—to see it clearly and accept it and be thankful for it—then any activity that helps us do that is worthwhile, and its form is the right form.

PB: Given that, what activities are you pursuing right now?

RA: The main thing we're doing is photographing clear-cuts. Most of the original forests in the Northwest have been destroyed, and no affirmation from the Northwest seems to me convincing if it can't acknowledge that fact. Will we get to a yes? Photographs are given, not taken, so we'll see.

Books are important to Kerstin and me, and we try to keep doing them. I've even, for fun, been carving some books out of wood. To have around the house instead of computer terminals.

An interview conducted in 2002 at the request of DoubleTake *magazine, but not printed before the magazine ceased publication. Peter Brown is a teacher, writer, and photographer; he has published two books of pictures:* Seasons of Light *and* On the Plains.

The only rule is that the wood has to have washed up on the beach.

PB: Do the books have text?

RA: One does. I asked Kerstin to calligraph on its open pages a line that Pablo Neruda wrote to his wife—"I made these sonnets out of wood." The rest of the books show just a horizon line. Have you read Mary Oliver's *The Leaf and the Cloud*? In it she asks: "would it be better to sit in silence?" Thankfully, her decision has been to speak, but for those of us who are not poets maybe a book of silence is permitted.

PB: My sense is that you and Kerstin are very much a team. And though I know you have strong feelings about privacy, tell me what you can about your photographic life together. How, for instance, do you work the clear-cuts?

RA: Kerstin and I share a lot of enthusiasms—Renaissance and Baroque music, for instance, and films. And we share concerns about population, environmental degradation, animal welfare, corporate misbehavior. . . . We're not saints. I give in to all kinds of despair and fury. But on the basis of our common enjoyments and commitments, we do get past some of these failures and go to work. Together. The mix changes some, and it's not always equal. Kerstin does all the cooking, for example, and I do almost all the photo business. What we share most is the editing, both of the pictures and of the text. She is very good.

Currently, she's going with me to industrial forests. The thought was to have somebody there in case I took a nosedive off a stump, like Darius Kinsey, but she's in a few of the pictures and I like them. One of my goals is to suggest the sadness of what has happened, and because she feels it, the way she stands or sits sometimes expresses a lot.

PB: Trees are central to much of your work. It seems to me that just as poets build up personal mythologies over time, photographers do the same. What do trees represent to you? Why are so many of your books focused on trees?

RA: The short answer, I suppose, is that they are so beautiful. But what does that mean? In Virginia Woolf's novel *To the Lighthouse* the central character, Mrs. Ramsay, thinks about three lines of poetry: "And all the lives we ever lived / And all the lives to be, / Are full of trees and changing leaves." That surely is a reason we attend to trees.

PB: Because trees are more than trees.

RA: Yes. Paul Tillich wrote, if I remember correctly, that everything we say about God, except this statement, is metaphor. Those are the likenesses I suppose I'm after. Never to be decoded. Left to stand.

With any metaphor, if one spells it out, not only the subject but the picture gets smaller.

Among the best things about photography is that by its nature it has to begin with specific cases. A tree is first of all wonderful as the particular tree it is. If it doesn't live for us in that way, then it's not going to take us further.

Though eventually, yes, a tree does point beyond itself. And our experience of it is enriched by associations and intuitions. A. J. Meek recently sent me an unforgettable view of the Union cemetery at Shiloh—rows of gravestones beneath old trees. The picture brings to mind Thomas Worthington Whittredge's painting of a camp meeting under trees. And Stonewall Jackson's dying words: "Let us cross over the river and rest under the shade of the trees." And George Barnard's pictures of trees broken by cannon fire. All those associations reinforce an understanding that the trees in Meek's picture are more than just landscaping.

PB: Trees often stand for people.

RA: Human beings and trees share some qualities. One quality that we do not share with trees, however, is our periodic inclination to gratuitous killing. Witness what we do to trees.

PB: You have implied elsewhere that you think nihilism underlies some of the practices of industrial forestry. Why do you believe that?

RA: Greed at first appears to account for clear-cutting, and that surely is a large part of it. But I'm suspicious. After people live a while in a place to which they've laid waste, it gets to be easy to hate a great many things. Including themselves. And anything green that tries to rise again.

PB: Your part of Colorado has changed dramatically over the years, and in many ways your work has been a documentation of the "laying waste" to that particular ground. Is this change the reason that you moved from Colorado to Oregon?

RA: Ironically, we moved to Oregon because we were tired. I felt I had seen too much for too long. And we had enjoyed living on the coast for short periods. But we had never paid attention to the interior of Oregon, and when we did that, our experience of the state changed. We discovered that only something like five percent of the old-growth forest remains. Most of the timber one sees now is a monoculture sustained by chemicals and harvested by clear-cutting, which is done in cycles of just thirty or forty years. And the timber industry has so thoroughly corrupted the social structure that it is hard to imagine how adequate change can come from within the region. The financing of Oregon's schools, for example, is linked directly to timber revenues, so to suggest that logging should be restricted—that clear-cutting should be stopped, for instance, before the soil is exhausted—is seen as an attack on children.

PB: Will these problems come out in your pictures?

RA: Not the complexities.

PB: What other issues bother you?

RA: More broadly, population. The American West is now seriously overpopulated and rapidly getting worse. It is an ecological
issue of the utmost consequence. Whole cities, for example, have
no future because there aren't sources of water to sustain them.
The most pressing problem is immigration. No matter where it
comes from—Boston or Mexico—it needs to be stopped.

    A friend recently passed along an essay by Garrett Hardin,
published over thirty years ago, titled "The Tragedy of the
Commons." In it, the author argues that accelerating environmental disaster mandates that ethics be two-tiered. Issues relating
just to human happiness—freedom to live anywhere we want,
freedom to have as many children as we want—must take second
place to issues of human survival and the survival of all life on
earth. It is an argument that raises frighteningly complex and
dangerous questions. But ours is not a privileged time.

PB: What sort of things would have to happen for Americans
seriously to consider such steps?

RA: Adequate education. Or the arrival of the Four Horsemen.

PB: You've been a photographer for over thirty-five years. Do you
work now for the same reasons, more or less, that you did at the
beginning?

RA: I still love the American West and I still love seeing an image
come up in the tray. If anything has changed it's that photography
seems harder. I'm less able to believe in the likelihood of economic

and social reform, a hope that once enabled me to photograph Denver streets. It's a problem that accompanies age, I assume.

PB: Are there compensations for age?

RA: Some. One comes to know friendship at its full value.

PB: You mentioned A. J. Meek. . . . I know that a good number of the photographers of my generation hold you in high regard and have been influenced both by your work and in some cases, by your friendship. You and Kerstin have no children of your own, but are in a way an almost familial (though distant) presence to many. I'd be interested in your comments on that thought.

RA: In important ways, it's the younger generation that keeps care of the older, giving it hope. I'm grateful. More than I can say, really.

PB: You have been very critical of America but you still love it. Why?

RA: Yeats wrote to Maud Gonne that "only God could love you for yourself alone and not your yellow hair." I love my country partly for itself alone, for its spirit, for its attempt to live up to the Declaration and the Constitution. But I also love America, almost to distraction, for what I see—for roads, fields, birds. . . .

PB: You've photographed the beauty and vulnerability of places that are often, on the surface at any rate, degraded—mostly the flatlands of the West, but also Los Angeles and now Oregon. Are there other parts of the country, or the world for that matter, that you would photograph, given time?

RA: I can't imagine any place that isn't worth photographing.

PB: In what ways have the events of September 11 changed your life?

RA: They've strengthened in me the sense that we are tragic. The attack did not perhaps need to happen. We'll never know. What we do know, I think, is that it would have been less likely if we had worked harder for social justice and world government. To do that, however, we would have had to be less selfish.

PB: How would you describe yourself politically?

RA: As a democratic socialist. Though given the realities of present-day America, I'll support almost anyone who works for equalizing access to television for all sides in an election. Many now in office are of course just shills for corporate power. They threaten our country more than the terrorists.

PB: Do you think we, as Americans, are worse than other people?

RA: Probably not. Maybe, just maybe, at times we've even been a little better than some. But that is small comfort as one looks at a child we've maimed in our effort to punish terrorists.

PB: Under the circumstances, what do you feel our obligations to be?

RA: Insofar as I understand them, to keep trying. And asking forgiveness.

PB: Your first book was on the rural churches of Colorado and your last was on a single piece of Buddhist sculpture. Does religion enter your life and thought in important ways?

RA: My impulse is to say yes, but that may seem unsupported when I add that I don't belong to any religious group, at least for now.

PB: Since September 11, life is harder for artists in the United States. They have even less support than before.

RA: In general, you're right. Perhaps saddest of all, it is harder for the young. To try to publish a first book, for example. Though as is so often the case, it could be worse. And our subject is still as compelling as ever. As Edward Dahlberg said: "Homer sang of many sacred towns in Hellas that were no better than Kansas City." I also try to remind myself of the obvious: no society has ever much encouraged the crazy notion that the way light falls on a vacant lot is important. Artists are dreamers.

PB: In a better world, what part might art play?

RA: It might help us know our dependency and express our gratitude. Artists would understand their work to be a calling. Museums would be places of focus and stillness.

PB: What pictures would you have in your ideal museum?

RA: If one chose well, one could build a wonderful collection around an etching by Rembrandt, a drawing by Cézanne, and a photograph by Atget.

PB: What sustains you visually in your own home?

RA: We actually have a print by Atget. And a treasured selection of photographs and paintings by colleagues. Together with the Gandharan sculpture that is the subject of the book you mentioned, and two New Mexican *santos*.

PB: What periodicals do you read? Do you subscribe to *DoubleTake*?

RA: I've subscribed from the beginning, and I hope for its long life, as I do for publications like the *New Yorker* and the *New York Review of Books*.

I've heard photographers say that *DoubleTake* favors writers, and I'm told that writers say it favors photographers. [laughs] If photographers have any truth on their side, it may in part reflect a problem built into magazine production—how to get a lot included, and make it lively, but at the same time present visual art, pictures that are complete in themselves. You could say that the problem is "who is going to be the artist, the photographer or the designer?" The difficulty arises particularly with the designer's use of bleeds (running the image to the edge of the page), and with the practice of extending pictures across the gutter. The four sides of the view in the camera finder are the photographer's main tools for bringing clarity out of life's confusion. If in a reproduction any of the sides of that frame are weakened, as happens with a bleed, or if the image is divided, the reproduction does not convey well the artist's primary gift to us.

My sense is that *DoubleTake* and *Aperture* and the publishers of photographic books must confront this problem if artists, as distinguished from journalists, are to be treated fairly.

PB: Do you read fiction?

RA: Very little anymore. But I do have a favorite novel: Virginia Woolf's *To the Lighthouse*. I wish I had time to commit large parts of it to memory.

PB: You've distinguished between photojournalism and art photography. What significance does the term "documentary" have for you?

RA: I wrestle with it, because so many of my heroes have been called documentarians—Timothy O'Sullivan, Eugène Atget, Lewis Hine, Dorothea Lange. . . . What do they have in common?

A commitment to a sustained, unblinking engagement with life, life in believable complexity. That's so hard to maintain that *documentary* always brings me back to the word *caring*. It's serious work.

PB: What do you work with? What are your photographic tools, and your thoughts on phototechnology in general? Does digital work hold interest for you? Computers?

RA: Anything is okay that works. I'm intrigued by the range of low-light conditions that seem open to digital cameras. And by any printmaking process that doesn't mandate breathing chemical fumes. And by any reproduction process that makes spotting easy. I am, however, alienated by the complexity of digital machinery, and by the apparently brief life expectancy of it. And by the doubtful longevity of the prints. There is, too, the obvious fact that an ink print is not the same as a silver gelatin print, even though they both may be beautiful and register an equal range of tones. I find that I still prefer gelatin silver prints, so I continue to use film cameras.

PB: One more question on trees. You've talked of Darius Kinsey, who photographed the logging—some might say *carnage*—of much of the old growth forests of the Northwest around the turn of the century. In considering his work now, in light of your own, what are your reactions?

RA: It just seems a completely different place now. Like a stage at the end of Act Five. Or maybe we're not quite there yet. As Margaret Drabble has reportedly observed, with wit: we're not at the beginning of the end, we're at the middle of the end.

PB: This has been a serious conversation.

RA: Yes, maybe too much so. Maybe we should return to Fran Lebowitz. She joked once, you know, that life seems "less like art than craft, less like a painting by Seurat than a macramé plant holder."

PB: That has the knottiness of life, even if it's a little short on the mystery.

RA: It's easy to neglect humor. And mystery too. There are so many astonishing encounters with mystery. I remember one foggy October evening, just after we had moved to Oregon, when we were sitting in the living room and Kerstin looked up from her reading and asked if I'd heard something. I hadn't. I listened and still couldn't be sure. She said it seemed to be coming from outside, so we opened the front door and went onto the porch, out into dense, dimly glowing fog. The sounds, we came to realize, were the voices of small birds migrating south over the hilltop on which we live, just out of sight up in the fog. They were perhaps no more than thirty or forty feet above us, but completely invisible. Their passage went on for a long time. How many thousands of birds must there have been? We never saw any of them but we could almost touch them. It was an event from which Charles Burchfield would have made a painting.

PB: What other reference points are important to you?

RA: Family and friends. Both those who are here now, and those who are no longer present in body. And some people whom I haven't ever met in person, and with whom I haven't even exchanged a letter, but whom I feel I know—Wendell Berry, Henry Beetle Hough, Edward Hopper, Emily Dickinson, Samuel Johnson. . . .

Even if one believes, as I do, that the general nature of life is suffering, there are still pleasures to be enjoyed. Eating at a beautifully set table, for example. And music. And working with hand tools—helping a chisel find the line of a boat or a bird or a book. Finding the shape in the wood.

ABOUT
THE BEST AND
THE WORST

WITH

ERIC PADDOCK

ERIC PADDOCK: What was the origin of your recent book *Turning Back*?

ROBERT ADAMS: In the 1980s I'd watched my father stand up in front of a hostile city council—he was in his eighties, and bent, and his hands shook—to ask that Astoria stop cutting its forests. Years later, when I visited him in the last months of his life, we talked about that again.

EP: Did Astoria stop cutting its trees?

RA: No. They've gotten a little more quiet about it.

EP: The book then is to speak for him?

RA: He never gave up. He did begin to laugh about it though. And not bitterly.

What I wanted to do in the book was to widen the subject to clear-cutting all across the Northwest. The problem for me in formulating the book was to find a way to tell the truth, but not to end in darkness.

Clear-cutting is going to lead to permanent deforestation, I believe, so I didn't want to include in the pictures of clear-cutting anything that might suggest a metaphor for regeneration— beautiful clouds or flowers or whatever. I don't believe that eventually there will be regeneration. What I wanted to record was an unforgivable crime. So the affirmation in *Turning Back*, and it is a measured one, is to be found in the book as a whole, not in any of the pictures of clear-cutting.

An interview conducted in the fall of 2005. Eric Paddock is a fifth-generation Coloradoan, a landscape photographer and writer and teacher, the creator of a photographic book about Colorado titled Belonging to the West, *and the Curator of Photography at the Colorado Historical Society. He and Adams have been friends for over twenty-five years.*

90

EP: What disappoints you most about America now?

RA: Its elevation of greed to a public virtue.

And the tyranny of popular culture—the widespread confusion of coarseness with strength, of loudness with significance, of novelty with value. On public radio, for example, Terry Gross spends hours discussing the minutiae of trash TV and movies. For which there is always this cost: those who think and create in more discriminating ways are left less understood and less supported, exactly where corporate America wants them to be left—marginalized, posing no threat to commercial advertising and political propaganda.

EP: What do you love most about America?

RA: Its artists, the real ones, those who work to produce art that will last a long time. Artists like Marilynne Robinson, the writer, who took over twenty years to complete the short novel *Gilead*, a book worthy of standing beside those by James and Faulkner. Or Kim Stafford, whose biography of his father, William Stafford, is an achievement in understanding no less than Boswell's.

EP: Where do the political calamities of recent years lead you? . . . The invasion of Iraq, the U.S. administration's endorsement of torture, its failure to engage the problem of global warming, the re-election—if that's what it was—of the Bush administration. . . .

RA: Torture is the most ominous development on that list, I think. Kerstin and I have, like many, thought about leaving, and we continue to think about it, although our age is an obstacle. The question is where. Kerstin is from Sweden, and we admire many of the values there, so we consider it, but the language is a barrier for me.

I had a Jewish teaching colleague who took the last train out of Germany. That's cutting it too close.

For any of us who stay, Anna Akhmatova's life and work establish a needed if almost impossible standard. She wrote: "One less hope means / One more song."

Some of Akhmatova's poetry was saved only because people memorized it—writing things down was too dangerous. There must have been a lot that was lost.

Though—and I can't explain this, but I do believe it—beautiful work is no less for a brief life. The language of religion has recently been debased, but I'll risk it. Art, along with some other caring activity, is prayer. Spoken and heard.

EP: If you were thirty again, what would you like to do?

RA: Lots of things. Remember when we used to talk about the fun it would be to start a postcard company? The cards were going to be the old-fashioned kind, with no type over the pictures. Just clear photographs of mostly everyday places. We could ask Ben and Mary and Bill and Ken and Willy and Chuck to help. We could do it.

EP: Maybe we should plan to give the cards away for the first few years, just to get things rolling.

RA: It must be time to follow the example of the Chilean poet Nicanor Parra, who ended every reading with the same statement: "I take back everything I told you." Time to grab a camera and check out those willows by the river. They were great in the spring, and they might even be better now in September.

ACKNOWLEDGMENTS

Designer Wendy Byrne and I have worked together since early in our professional lives. This volume, like others before it, was made possible by her kindness, skill, and caring.

I am also indebted to my editor, Diana Stoll, for helping me try to be clear and civilized, and for her sense of humor.

The staff at Aperture made arrangements for the book a pleasure. Special thanks go to Michael Famighetti, Melissa Harris, and Bryonie Wise.

Thanks also to Richard Woodward for his Foreword.

Not least, I am grateful, as I have been on many earlier occasions, to friends Lynne and Harold Honickman.